—

BYRNES HIGH SCHOOL FOOTBALL

GRIDIRON HISTORY

ZACHARY JOHNSON

Charleston | London

THE
History
PRESS

Published by The History Press
Charleston, SC 29403
www.historypress.net

First published 2010

Manufactured in the United States

ISBN 978.1.60949.169.7

Library of Congress Cataloging-in-Publication Data

Johnson, Zachary (Zachary David), 1981-
Byrnes High School football : rebels gridiron history / Zachary Johnson.
p. cm.
ISBN 978-1-60949-169-7
1. James F. Byrnes High School (Duncan, S.C.)--Football--History. 2. Football-
-South Carolina--Duncan--History. 3. School sports--South Carolina--Duncan-
-History. 4. High school football players--South Carolina--Duncan--History. 5.
Duncan (S.C.)--Social life and customs. I. Title.

GV959.53.D86J64 2010
796.332'620975729--dc22

2010043797

A view of Nixon Field from the visitors' side. *Courtesy of Ronnie Black.*

The people of our district have always exhibited a spirit of loyalty and sacrifice unsurpassed by those anywhere and it is the hope of those of us who "carry on" that we prove worthy of the traditions of the past and the rich heritage is ours to uphold.
—*D.M. Nixon, 1936*

CONTENTS

CONTENTS

CONTENTS

PREFACE

As we approach the fifty-fifth anniversary of James F. Byrnes High School, we should all take the time to reflect on the history behind the school we hold so close to our hearts. It is, after all, the home of our beloved Rebels.

With great respect to all of our athletic programs, it's the football team that has helped create a common bond between those folks who live in the District 5 community. Every Friday night starting in the fall and ending in December, people from every background, denomination and social class gather at Nixon Field to cheer on the mighty Rebels.

Although our recent dominance over South Carolina football started in 2002, the Rebels have been a football power since the beginning. From their first playoff appearance in 1955 to their 2008 state championship, Byrnes has posted a 413–230–18 all-time record, with twenty-five appearances in the playoffs and nine state championships.

But the success that we enjoy today did not come overnight. The foundation was set in place generations ago by folks who have long since passed and by some who are still with us today. The history and future of Byrnes football is all around District 5; you don't need to look hard to see it. If you would like to meet some of the 1955

Rebels, walk around the home side and you'll find a few of them. If you would like to see future Rebels before they become stars, catch a D.R. Hill or Florence Chapel game.

It is the hope that this book will rekindle the memories of events and locations long forgotten. At one point, our community had three high schools. The consolidation in 1950 combined Duncan High School, Reidville High School and WLT High into the creation of District 5. The consolidation eventually led to the creation of James F. Byrnes High in 1955. In 1968, Florence Chapel High School and Byrnes were integrated.

This anthology is for those fortunate enough to have grown up in this community, for all of those that hold the honor of being educated in District 5 Schools of Spartanburg and for those who like to learn why the Rebels are so loved in District 5.

ACKNOWLEDGEMENTS

THANKS!
This publication would not be possible without the input of various individuals. If not for their donations, interviews and memories, this project would have never made it to print. Thank you.

Frank Cook (Duncan, class of 1951)
Choice Watson (WLT, class of 1951)
Helen Ruth Dawkins (Florence Chapel, class of 1956)
Willie Dawkins (Florence Chapel, class of 1957)
Gerald Turner (Byrnes, class of 1957)
Charlie Clayton (Byrnes, class of 1957)
James "Bo" Corne (Byrnes, class of 1961)
Ray Johnson (Byrnes, class of 1970)
Randy Dill (Byrnes, class of 1971)
Ronnie Black (Byrnes, class of 1971)
Tony McAbee (Byrnes, class of 1980)
Bobby Bentley (Byrnes, class of 1986)
Chris Courtney (Byrnes, class of 1986)
Brad Watson (Byrnes, class of 1989)
Tony Gillespie (Byrnes, class of 1990)
"Darth Rebel" (Byrnes, class of 1993)

Rebels celebrate after winning the 1976 championship. *Courtesy of Byrnes High School.*

Austin Barnett (Byrnes, class of 1997)
Chris Miller
Joel Fitzpatrick
James F. Byrnes High School
James F. Byrnes Athletic Department
District 5 Schools of Spartanburg County

CHAPTER 1

BEFORE THERE
WAS BYRNES

DISTRICT 5'S CONSOLIDATION

The reorganization of Spartanburg school districts became effective on July 1, 1950. The consolidation of various schools was a direct result of a special election that was held in October 1949. The resulting bill stated that "School District No. 5 shall be the area now comprising school districts known as Zoar No. 1, Fairmont No. 24, Reidville No. 43, Wellford No. 48, Abner Creek No. 59, Startex No. 60, Frey No. 71, Henson No. 73, Duncan No. 75, Ballenger No. 96, Woods Chapel No. 98, Lyman No. 100, and Poplar Springs No. 64."

James Byrnes, along with other South Carolina political minds, spearheaded the renaissance of public education in South Carolina. It was through their actions and campaigning while serving their state that the leaders in education began to rethink how education was provided.

District 5 has grown by leaps and bounds. Despite its growth over the years, the communities that make up our district still have a "small town" atmosphere.

Here is a short time line of the district:

1950 District 5 is founded.
1955 James F. Byrnes is established.
1955 Florence Chapel is established.
1963 Former District 5 High building is named D.R. Hill Junior High.
1968 Florence Chapel fully integrates with Byrnes.
1974 New D.R. Hill Middle opens.
2004 Florence Chapel Middle School opens.
2006 New D.R. Hill opens.
2006 Old D.R. Hill is converted into Byrnes Freshman Academy.

WLT High School

Founded in 1928, WLT provided education for those who lived in the Wellford, Lyman and Tucapau (now known as Startex) communities. Students who lived as far as modern-day Fairmont and Brookside Village would have also attended the school. WLT was the smallest school in the Middle Tyger area, but according to alumni, the school was the most ferocious in spirit.

The Wildcats, dressed in blue and gold, traveled across the state to face schools of relative size. Just like their descendants (Byrnes), WLT was never afraid of competing against larger high schools. Some of these schools included Landrum, Williamston, Chesnee and crosstown rival Duncan.

If WLT had a rival, it most certainly would be the Indians of Duncan High School. Duncan and WLT met annually to decide who would have bragging rights. According to records, WLT came out on top most of the time. Some WLT grads have said that "Duncan had a bigger squad with more students to choose from, but WLT had the athletes." Perhaps their most memorable game against Duncan was in 1947. WLT won that game 26–20, securing the District 11 Class B championship.

Usually, the teams that WLT played were also from small mill towns with multigrade schoolhouses. But being a small school did not mean that WLT lacked fan support. When competing at home

WLT head coach O.A.
Tucker with a couple
of his players in 1943.
Courtesy of Choice Watson.

The 1941 WLT Wildcats, co-state football champions. *Courtesy of Choice Watson.*

(located across the street from Lyman Methodist Church on the lot that now houses storage buildings built by Springs), fans would fill the bleachers' capacity to cheer on the Wildcats. Like modern-day games, WLT's games featured a pep band, cheerleaders and concessions. However, the most notable absence would have been the safety standards seen today, such as facemasks on helmets.

Despite its closing long ago, WLT's legacy has not been forgotten. We have a solid foundation with football in District 5, and WLT is a part of that foundation. In closing, here is a little-known fact: the 1941 WLT Wildcats were named South Carolina co-state champions. They finished that season with a 6–0–1 record.

Duncan High School

With a mascot that would make any Gaffney fan smile, the black and gold Indians of Duncan High School were prototypes of what became Byrnes High. Built in 1927 at a cost of $85,000, Duncan High School served students in the old Spartanburg School District 75.

If you could go back to Duncan High today, the athletics department would have obvious similarities and peculiar differences. The similarities would include a bitter rivalry with Fairforest (Dorman); school colors that are still used today at D.R. Hill (black and gold); and very strong community support. Perhaps the biggest difference would be the Indian mascot.

On game days, people from all over town would show up and pack the wooden stands to see Duncan face teams from Boiling Springs, Union, Fairforest and WLT. At a cost of $5,000, the football field was completed in 1929. At the time, Duncan's field was considered a gem among football fields in the county. For instance, the Indians' football field was the first in the county to be equipped for night games after having lights installed before the 1948 season. Duncan's field also featured a hand-operated scoreboard, a section for the band in the stands and a privacy fence that ran the length of the field. The site of the old football field can still be seen today, but now standing in its place is the Shipwreck Cove Water Park.

Duncan High linemen in 1949. *Courtesy of Choice Watson.*

The consolidation of the schools in District 5 eventually led to the closing of Duncan High. However, this did not bring about the end of Indian football in Duncan. Until 1954, the athletes of WLT and Duncan continued using the colors and nickname of Duncan High until the opening of Byrnes. Together, they were known as the District 5 Indians.

Today, the colors and spirit of Duncan High live on through the black and gold Tigers of D.R Hill.

District 5 High School

Athletes of the newly consolidated District 5 were establishing traditions and foundations for years to come. All school athletics were now under the guise of District 5 athletics. From the 1950 season onward, all athletes would be known as the District 5 Indians.

Combining the athletes from WLT and Duncan met with great success, and the "new" Indians of District 5 entered the 1950 football season with high expectations. District 5 featured an all-star

A game between Greer and District 5 High in 1952. District 5 is wearing the dark jerseys. *Courtesy of Choice Watson.*

cast of players and coaches that first year. Gilbert Cox, who served as head coach at WLT, took over as head coach and athletic director of District 5 schools. Nelson Schofield, the head coach of Duncan the previous year, stepped down as the offensive and defensive line coach. A third assistant, James Hill, rounded out the trio. For the past two seasons, Coach Cox's Wildcats of WLT had laid claim to the District 11 Class B Championship, and with that success came high expectations for the newly consolidated football team.

The Indians kicked off the 1950 season with a 46–13 win over Pacolet. Other key games that season included wins over Woodruff, Greer and a tie with Fairforest (Dorman). The Indians would finish the 1950 season with an impressive 8–2–1 record. Coach Cox would leave District 5 after the 1950 season, and Nelson Schofield would eventually take over as head coach shortly thereafter. With the 1950 football season came a standard of success in football that is still carried on today. The Indians would only be around for four more seasons. With the conclusion of the 1954 season came the beginning of a new era of football in our district—the Rebel football era.

In 1955, the three-story building where the Indians played their home games was renamed Duncan Junior High School. From 1963 until 1974, it was called **D.R. Hill Junior High School**, in memory of the first and only superintendent of Duncan High School. For ten years, the building stood vacant, slowly decomposing and becoming a hazard. The District 5 School Board decided to level the building in 1984 at a cost of $46,000.

Florence Chapel High School

For those growing up in District 5 now, segregation may seem unrealistic. But segregation was a reality during the mid-twentieth century, and as unfortunate as it may seem, District 5 had segregated school populations. Based in the former WLT High School building in Wellford, Florence Chapel School for fourteen years served the African Americans of District 5 from grades one through twelve. Florence Chapel's spirit still lives on today through its alumni and those in the community who choose not to forget about the "Fighting Hornets."

Florence Chapel fielded nearly every type of sport, including basketball, baseball and football. None of the three main sports was more popular than the other, but graduates tend to remember the football games more than the other sports. The stands were usually packed when the Hornets played. With teams such as Beck and Washington (Greenville) on the slate, Florence Chapel never had it easy.

According to Helen Ruth Dawkins (class of 1956) Florence Chapel "always put up a fight on the football field." Ms. Dawkins went on to say that regardless of whether Florence Chapel won, "the games were always fun to attend." Willie Dawkins added that if there was one team to beat, it was the Lincoln Rattlers (Taylors, South Carolina); they were the main rivals. He said that "Lincoln was the bigger team. We weren't supposed to beat them, and if we did, they would want to fight." Willie Dawkins went on to say that "when we played Lincoln under the (stadium lights) nearly 800 to a 1,000 fans would show up to watch the game."

A couple of years before desegregation was final, District 5 schools began to integrate the students by trying something unique.

In an effort to make the transition as smooth as possible, in 1966, a handful of students from Florence Chapel were brought into the white schools. While some schools in the state and county were experiencing turmoil over desegregation, District 5 had few problems. Ray Johnson (Byrnes class of 1970) said that "some of us were already friends. We had already been playing baseball with some of the students from Florence Chapel before '66 at the old Fairmont baseball field. We were excited to have the athletes from Florence Chapel; we thought desegregation was long overdue." With desegregation came Byrnes's first African American football player, Curtis Baker. Baker, a sophomore when brought in, is fondly remembered by his teammates as being a great athlete, a great friend and "fast as all get-out."

By 1969, segregation was abolished in District 5, and in the same year came the closing of Florence Chapel. Forty years later people still remember their days as a Hornet. Willie Dawkins's fondest memories there were the teachers and the discipline. He said that "the teachers were like moms away from home, and the discipline is just something that is not taught these days."

In 2004, the newly built middle school was named in honor of the old Florence Chapel.

CHAPTER 2
EST. 1955

The First Year

Opening its doors in 1955 to about five hundred students, James F. Byrnes High School's creation was the eventual result of the consolidation of Spartanburg County schools. Today, despite doubling in size, relocating the freshman and having three times the amount of students, Byrnes remains a close-knit school in the center of District 5.

Most of Byrnes's traditions were cemented back in 1955. According to Gerald Turner (Byrnes class of 1958), it was the student body that voted on the school colors, the "Rebels" nickname and the name of the school. The student body was given the opportunity to give Byrnes its identity.

When voting, students were given a selection of names to choose from in regard to the school name. History has since forgotten what some of those names were, but James F. Byrnes was the winner. Next on the ballot were the school colors and mascot. A combination of colors and potential mascots were given for the students to choose from. With an overwhelming majority of the votes, the nickname Rebels won, along with the colors of blue and gray.

Of course, you can't go without a fight song. And although Byrnes kicked off its first football season in 1955, the song "Rebel Rouser" by Duane Eddy did not debut until 1958, shortly after the school adopted the song as its own. Like every school, Byrnes needed an alma mater. Byrnes teacher Hazel Allison, with the help of Mildred Simpson, wrote the alma mater in 1955:

Alma Mater

Neath these Carolina Skies
On Earth's fairest land;
Hear our alma mater lies
Held in God's own Hands.
May His Blessings keep thee safe
May thy Children be
True to these ideals we've learned
James Byrnes High from Thee.

Here within these Sheltering walls
Knowledge rules supreme;
Here we've lighted friendship fires.
Shared in youth's brightest dream
Here the future meets today!
This is our pledge shall be;
Faith in God and Freedoms way.
Strength in liberty.

Once across the quiet land
Winds of hatred blew.
War Clouds thundered death upon
Boys in Gray and Blue.
Raise Byrnes High School banner high
See the blue and gray
Joined at last in one proud flag
Symbol of today.

Though your children travel far,
We'll remember still
Dreaming Carolina Skies;

Peaceful Southern Hills,
Where a Rebel standard flies
Proudly floating free—
Then our pledge we'll give a new;
James Byrnes High to thee.

Chorus:
To our alma mater brings songs
Of love and praise;
Grateful hearts will not forget
Happy high school days…
Rally round the gray and blue
Sound the Rebel cry!
Loyal sons and daughters true

Many of the traditions established that first year are still with us today. Byrnes graduates have always shown a respect for the school's traditions, and it's that same respect that has kept the school at the forefront for many years. Byrnes is more than just a place where students excel in athletics; it's a place that teaches young men and women the foundations needed in order to be successful.

Byrnes is a school with many blessings, and its graduates are perhaps some of the proudest alumni in America. To see this pride, come to a football game and notice crowds numbering in the thousands in attendance. Why is this a sign of pride? It's because the crowds usually outnumber the student population.

JAMES F. BYRNES

U.S. Senator, 1931–41; Supreme Court Justice, 1941–2;
Secretary of State, 1945–7; Governor of South Carolina 1951–5

As congressman and senator, James Byrnes demonstrated outstanding talents and was acclaimed generally as the most effective legislator of his day.

With distinction, he sat on our highest court but unhesitatingly resigned to devote himself selflessly first as a war mobilizer for World War II and later as secretary of state to direct our foreign policy toward the goal of world peace. In all these undertakings, he reflected credit and honor on his native state and on himself.

Our school honors him specially, though, because as governor of South Carolina, he fathered an educational renaissance in his native state, the benefits of which will endure as long as South Carolina.

When traveling through our state, you will get a glimpse of the Byrnes name in several locations. While traveling though Spartanburg, you will most likely take a ride down the James F. Byrnes Memorial Highway. The James F. Byrnes Academy, another school in South Carolina, was been named after him. A street in Columbia and a dorm at Clemson University shares his name as well.

If Byrnes were still alive today, he would definitely be proud of our school and all of its accomplishments.

D.M. NIXON

Nixon Who? Nixon Field!

D.M. Nixon Field (better known as Nixon Field) is perhaps the most central character of Rebel football. Every Friday night from late summer to late November, fans congregate inside the stadium to support the Byrnes Rebels and listen to the Rebel Regiment. Nixon Field is the place that everyone wants to be on Friday nights. Nixon even has a pep group named after it, the "Nixon Nuts."

Drury M. Nixon, 1952

So who was Nixon Field named for? Contrary to what some people believe, the field was not named after the former commander in chief.

Drury M. Nixon Jr. was the superintendent of the WLT school district for years. He was very supportive of athletics and did whatever he had to do to ensure that the school teams were well funded. When the schools were consolidated in the area that is now known as District 5, Nixon was named superintendent of its high schools, which included D5 High and Florence Chapel High School.

After the consolidation of the schools, it was only a couple of years until a new high school was built (the school we love, now named Byrnes). When construction of Byrnes was in the finishing stages, the general feeling among the D5 administration was that, instead of spending the money on a new football field, the Byrnes Rebels would play on the old WLT football field (formerly located across the street from Lyman Methodist, Springs warehouses now sit on top of the old location). Nixon was adamantly opposed to this and thought that the football field should be located on the school's campus. After much deliberation and politicking, D.M. Nixon won the support he needed, and Byrnes had a football field on its campus.

While it's not the newest field, Byrnes has one of the finest stadiums in the state. If D.M. Nixon were alive today, he would be very proud of the place that bears his name. Not much has changed at Nixon Field since 1955. Sure, there have been several renovations around the field and to the school, but unlike many schools, we still play football at the same site as we did when we opened.

There have been various facelifts at Nixon Field over the years. Most notable would be where the home fans sit. Until 1979, Byrnes fans sat in what is now the visitors' stands, and the visiting stands sat where the home stands are now. Other differences are that the scoreboard was once hand operated; a track once circled the football field; the restrooms past the east end zone were once a concession stand and served as the offices of the Byrnes Booster Club; and trees once surrounded the west end zone.

Combined with a state-of-the-art field house, the JumboTron, excellent field maintenance and professional-quality field art, it is no wonder Nixon Field is a gem among high school stadiums. It is cherished by all of those who have played on it and by those who attend.

THE INAUGURAL SEASON

Inside a brand-new, $75,000 stadium, the Byrnes Rebels kicked off their inaugural season on September 10, 1955. With Head Coach Charlie Burnett at the helm, the Rebs avoided a loss by virtue of a tie with the visiting Blue Eagles of Clover. Despite Byrnes marching deep into Clover's territory numerous times, the Rebs were not able to score a touchdown.

That game was the first of many legendary games to be played at Byrnes. The Rebels would go on to finish with a respectable six wins, three losses and two ties with an appearance in the playoffs. The momentum set forth that first year would set the Rebels up to have many successful seasons to come. Little did the fans know that they were getting a glimpse at the foundation of one of the most storied programs in South Carolina history.

1955 (6–3–2)

Byrnes	2	Clover	2
	43	Blue Ridge	13
	31	Boiling Springs	6
	19	Fairforest (Dorman)	13
	0	Woodruff	0
	20	Cowpens	12
	0	Laurens	6
	26	Chapman	7
	13	Travelers Rest	6
	12	Greer	60
	12	Olympia	32

LONG AGO, BUT NOT FORGOTTEN

With time, the memories of the events have almost been forgotten. For instance, Gerald Turner (class of 1958) recalled some tension between Byrnes and Chapman during the preseason. "Charlie Burnett coached the previous season at Chapman, and some of the fans and athletes did not appreciate him leaving," said Turner. He mentioned that before the game between Chapman and Byrnes, some of the Chapman faithful came to Nixon Field and painted vulgarities on the press box and field. "Coach Burnett was furious; he jokingly made a bet with us, saying that if we score 100 points on them (Chapman) he would give us his entire paycheck. So, at kickoff, the Rebels came out and played a great game. By the end of the first quarter we were on top 20–0." Turner says that Coach Burnett was getting a little nervous about having to possibly dish out his paycheck. Byrnes won that game 26–7.

Another fun piece of history happened the week of Byrnes's opening football game. On Tuesday, September 6, 1955, the Lions Club of Spartanburg hosted a preseason jamboree. The jamboree was broken up into twelve-minute scrimmages. Those scrimmages included a Wofford College intrasquad scrimmage, District 6 versus Cowpens, Woodruff versus Greer, Chapman versus Byrnes and, in the finale, the Spartanburg (Crimson Tide) Reds versus Blacks.

Some of the "Original Rebels" reunited at a home game in 2005. *Courtesy of Tony MacAbee.*

The only touchdown to be scored during the entire jamboree was by District 6. Aside from the football exhibitions, the festivities also included a beauty contest and a one-hundred-yard dash between selected members from each football team. The race had a stipulation stating that "each participant must wear his entire uniform." Ken Waddell of Byrnes was the winner and was thereby named the "fastest football player in the state" by the judges.

In 2005, the '55 Rebels were honored during homecoming. Coach Burnette, now living in Charleston, was also on hand that night.

Some of the "Original Rebels" reunited at a home game in 2005.

CHAPTER 3

THE COACHES

Byrnes has had ten head coaches guide the football team over the years. While some have been more successful than others, the fact remains that Byrnes can lay claim to having some of the finest head coaches of its time. In the following section, you will find brief summaries on each of the head coaches.

CHARLES BURNETTE

1955

In his first and only season as the head coach of the Rebels, Charles Burnette led the Rebels to a 6–3–2 finish.

H.L. QUINTANA

1956–8

Some of Coach Quintana's surviving players have said he is most remembered for the 1956 Woodruff game.

In that game, Byrnes led the eventual 1956 Class A State Champions 6–0 late in the game. Because of a turnover deep in Rebel territory, the Wolverines were able to score a touchdown and make the PAT. The final score in that game was 7–6. Quintana was 17–11–5 at Byrnes.

JOE HAZLE

1959–65

Coach Hazle made an immediate impact his first year at Byrnes, finishing 7–3–1. In all of his seasons at Byrnes, he finished with a 30–20–5 record. It was during Hazle's tenure that the Rebels would experience a lot of "firsts" as a program:

Coach Joe Hazle. *Courtesy of Byrnes High School.*

(1) First to defeat Woodruff (1959, 6–0);
(2) First to defeat Greer (1959, 7–6);
(3) First to defeat Spartanburg (1961, 19–0);
(4) First to defeat Dorman (1963, 20–0);
(5) First losing season (1962);
(6) First team to reach nine wins in a season (1963).

The 1962 season was a rebuilding year for the Rebels, finishing 2–7–1. However, the next two seasons would provide a remedy, as Byrnes finished 9–2 and 8–4.

KERMIT LITTLEFIELD

1966–7

Coach Littlefield holds the dubious distinction of having the fewest wins as head coach of Byrnes.

After the 1966 season, Coach Littlefield stepped down as head coach. Littlefield was 5–15–2 at Byrnes.

DALTON RIVERS

1968–76

Head Coach Dalton Rivers in 1969. *Courtesy of Byrnes High School.*

Rivers ended his career at Byrnes on top, finishing with only one other losing season (1971) and with the school's first state title in football.

With an all-star team loaded with talent that included Mike Glenn, Bill Smith and Steve Durham, Coach Rivers and the Rebels brought home the 3-AAA championship in 1976. Byrnes's final record that year was 12–1–1.

Coach Rivers left Byrnes after the 1976 championship season and took a head coach job at Broome High School. He was 65–32–4 at Byrnes.

JAMES "BO" CORNE

1977–86

After working under Dalton Rivers since the 1970 season, Bo Corne was promoted to head coach after Rivers's departure. He holds the distinction of being the first Byrnes alumnus to become head coach.

Corne won two state titles during his tenure. The first, in 1982, came by a 9–6 win over Myrtle Beach in the 3-AAA finals at Nixon Field. Corne and the Rebels competed for the school's third state title in 1985 when a young Bobby Bentley led the

Coach James "Bo" Corne. *Courtesy of Byrnes High School.*

Rebels to a 10–4 finish. The Rebels would come up short, though, losing 14–13 in the 4-AAAA final against Hillcrest-Dalzell.

In 1986—Coach Corne's last season as head coach—Byrnes went to the state finals a second year in a row and won the 4-AAAA Division II title in a 41–14 victory over Berkeley. The Rebels finished the 1986 season with an 11–3 record. Corne finished his career in education at Byrnes as assistant principal. Currently, he holds an elected seat as a member of the District 5 School Board. Corne was 76–38–2 at Byrnes.

KEITH MCALLISTER

1987–8

Coach McAlister came to Byrnes after being head coach at Strom Thurmond High School. While at Thurmond, he had a 91–20 record, six region titles and three appearances in the 3-AAA state championship finals.

McAlister was only at Byrnes two short seasons, finishing 6–5 both years. He was 12–10 at Byrnes.

FRED COAN

1989–94

After a two-year absence from the playoffs, Coan led the Rebels back to the post season in his first year as head coach.

While head coach, Coan's Rebels made three appearances in the playoffs and claimed one region title. He stepped down as head coach in 1994 and became the Byrnes athletic director. Coan was 34–35 at Byrnes.

BOBBY BENTLEY

1995–2006

In the summer of 1983, Coach Tommy Woodward saw the potential in Bentley after watching him play baseball. Woodward approached him shortly thereafter about playing football; the rest is history.

After graduating from Presbyterian College, Bentley returned to Byrnes in 1990 as an assistant coach. When Coach Coan became the athletic director following the '94 season, Bentley was named shortly after as the new head coach of the Rebels.

Despite finishing 2–9 and 1–11 in his first two seasons at the helm, the 1997 season showed a glimpse of things to come when the Rebels won their first playoff game in eleven seasons. Bentley would only have one more losing season during his tenure.

In the years to come, Bentley's teams would break many state records (team and individual), win four state titles in a row, rise to national prominence and would be regarded as one of the best programs in America. Coach Bentley's record during his last five years as head coach was 68–4.

When the 2006 season ended, Bentley resigned from Byrnes to become the head coach of Presbyterian College. After spending two seasons at the helm of PC (guiding the Blue Hose to a successful season in their first year as a Division I school), Bentley returned home. Coach Bentley now serves as the District 5 public relations director, the districtwide athletic director and offensive coordinator for the Rebels. His complete record at Byrnes was 107–52.

Coach Bobby Bentley with the trophy Byrnes won at the Kirk Herbstreet Ohio vs. USA invitational in 2006. *Courtesy of Byrnes High School.*

CHRIS MILLER

2007–present

Head Coach Chris Miller.
Courtesy of Byrnes High School.

Taking over a head coaching job can be stressful, especially in a program with such stellar expectations. Coach Bentley left behind a team that had won four state titles in a row, been ranked nationally and, arguably, was one of the best teams in state history.

The community nervously waited to find out who would be the next coach.

In January 2007, a giant sigh of relief could be heard as Chris Miller was named the new head coach.

Miller, a standout athlete at Wade Hampton High School and Newberry College, seemed like the perfect fit for Byrnes. After all, his first job was as an assistant coach was at Byrnes, when he coached from 1982 to 1986 for Bo Corne.

After leaving Byrnes, Miller went to Broome High School, where he was named head coach after being an assistant for only four seasons. While at Broome, his teams made the playoffs and won a region championship, and he was once named the *Herald-Journal* Coach of the Year.

Following the 1997 season, Miller went to Spartanburg High School, where he spent six years with the Vikings. Coach Miller returned to Byrnes in 2004 when he was named defensive coordinator and associate head coach.

Possessing the best defensive mind in the state, Coach Miller has continued the winning tradition at Byrnes, going 15–0 his first year as head coach and snagging back-to-back state titles. His record, so far, is 50–6.

Coaches' Record Summary, 1955–Present

Charles Burnett

Overall record: 6–3–2.
Won first game as coach? No; tied Clover 2–2.
Playoff appearances: 0.

H.L. Quintana

Overall record: 17–11–5.
Record first season: 7–3.
Won first game as coach? Yes; beat Clover 25–13.
Playoff appearances: 0.
Record last season as coach: 5–4–1.

Joe Hazle

Overall record: 30–20–5.
Record first season: 7–3–1.
Won first game as coach? No; tied Spartanburg 0–0.
Playoff appearances: 1.
Record last season as coach: 3–7–1.

Kermit Littlefield

Overall record: 5–15–2.
Record first season: 2–8–1.
Won first game as coach? No; lost to Pickens 18–0.
Playoff appearances: 0.
Record last season as coach: 3–7–1.

Dalton Rivers

Overall record: 65–32–4.
Record first season: 7–4.
Won first game as coach? Yes; beat Seneca 20–0.
Playoff appearances: 2 (1975, 1976).
Record last season as coach: 12–1–1 (1976 3-AAA State Champions).

Bo Corne

Overall record: 76–38–2.
Record first season: 3–6–1.
Won first game as coach? No; lost to Dorman 7–0.
Playoff appearances: 5 (1982, 1983, 1984, 1985, 1986).
Record last season as coach: 11–3 (1986 4-AAAA State Champions).

Keith McAlister

Overall record: 12–10.
Record first season: 7–6.
Won first game as coach? Yes; beat Greer 22–21.
Playoff appearances: 1 (1987).
Record last season as coach: 7–6.

Fred Coan

Overall record: 34–35.
Record first season: 3–6–1.
Won first game as coach? No; lost to Dorman 7–0.
Playoff appearances: 3 (1989, 1993, 1994).
Record last season as coach: 6–6.

The Coaches

Bobby Bentley

Overall record: 107–52.

Record first season: 2–9.

Won first game as coach? No; lost to Greer 38–7.

Playoff appearances:10 (1996, 1997, 1998, 2000, 2001, 2002, 2003, 2004, 2005, 2006).

Record last season as coach: 11–2 (Won four state titles in a row as head coach).

Chris Miller

Overall record: 50–6.

Record first season: 15–0.

Won first game as coach? Yes; beat Hartsville 55–28.

Playoff appearances: 4 (2007, 2008, 2009, 2010).

Record during 2009 season: 13–2 (Won two state titles as head coach).

CHAPTER 4
LEADING THE CHARGE

CHAMPIONSHIP-WINNING COACHES

Think back on your playing career. Whether you played football or some other sport, you had a head coach. Head coaches are supposed to be leaders in their school and community and take you to levels of competition that could not be reached on your own. For most, head coaches hold a special place in athletes' hearts. The same can be said about most of the former head coaches at Byrnes High School.

So, if Byrnes High is a measuring stick on tradition and winning ways and is a school where only the best men in the state are hired to take the helm, then the man hired as head coach should be the best of the best, right? You bet! Four out of the ten head coaches at Byrnes have won a state championship in football. Three of those men have won the title more than once. That means that "Rebel Pride & Tradition" has carried over for generations and has not been something that has happened overnight.

The Rebels have been blessed to have such a fine group of leaders over the years. In District 5, you cannot mention the names Rivers, Corne, Bentley and Miller without invoking a series of debates on "which one was better" or "do you remember that game when coach called…" The fact remains that not only are the four coaches mentioned here the greatest coaches in Byrnes football history, but they are also regarded as some of the best coaches of all time in the Palmetto State.

There are some common bonds between the men in this section. Perhaps it is those bonds that made them the coaches they became. Not just anyone can be a head coach. It takes someone with leadership skills, compassion, thick skin and the ability to take players where they have never been before. In the last section, you were given a glimpse of all of the head coaches who have journeyed through Byrnes. However, this section will provide a detailed look at the ones who truly separated themselves from the pack.

Some of the fun facts you will pick up is the connection Broome and Byrnes shares—not just with one coach but two coaches; also how another local high school could have landed one of the most innovative offensive coaches but lost him. Another nugget would be that at one point, Byrnes had the youngest 4-AAAA head coach in the state.

I had the pleasure to sit down and chat with the championship-winning coaches. It was enlightening to discover the similarities all of these men shared. Growing up, I remember hearing about one of the coaches (Rivers) from my father, sitting in the principal's office of another (Corne), playing for one (Bentley) and working for the last (Miller). As you read this section, I hope it brings back memories of your playing days, and hopefully you will discover things you never knew before about these remarkable coaches.

DALTON RIVERS

Growing up in rural Chesterfield County, Dalton Rivers graduated from Chesterfield High School in 1953. An all-conference athlete, Rivers was given the opportunity to continue his playing career in college.

"Tiger"

Rivers began his college playing career as a Clemson Tiger in 1953. Playing for the legendary Frank Howard, Rivers had the distinction of being on the first Tigers squad to compete in the ACC, which was established in 1953. While Rivers was at Clemson, the Tigers record improved every season, finishing 3–5–1, 5–5, 7–3 and 7–2–2, respectively. When looking back at his Clemson days, Rivers fondly recalled that "although we lost the Orange Bowl (to Colorado 27–21) we won Clemson's first-ever ACC title my senior year; that meant a lot to us."

Early Success

Upon graduation, Rivers served six months' active duty in the army and served the five and a half months remaining in the reserves. After fulfilling his six months of active duty, Rivers was hired at Lancaster High School prior to the 1958 football season. Early in his coaching career, Rivers found a taste for success. In 1958, the Lancaster Hurricanes, led by Head Coach Wade Corn and a group of talented assistants, including Rivers, won the AA state championship. "The win was huge for the community," remarked Rivers. "The previous year, Lancaster had lost the state title to North Augusta. So yeah, to come back that next year was huge; and as a first year assistant coach, it meant a lot to me." Coach Rivers would stay in Lancaster one more season before making a life-changing decision.

From Sideline to Textiles

After spending two seasons living his dream, Coach Rivers decided to hang up the whistle and move onto a more profitable profession. After making up his mind to leave education, Rivers took a job in 1960 with textiles, working at J.P. Stevens in Great Falls, South Carolina. "At the time, I was tired of not making much money. As everyone knows, there isn't much money in coaching," says Rivers about his decision.

Working in the front office, Dalton continued to think about football. It wasn't long before the desire proved to be too strong. Rivers said that he "wanted to be back on the sidelines; I missed it." In the spring of 1962, Rivers left J.P. Stevens and went back into coaching.

Down the Road Again

After a two-year hiatus, Coach Rivers returned to coaching. This time, however, Rivers found himself at Chester High School. Hired by Chester head coach R.E. Wilson, Rivers walked into a program that had not found much success in recent years. Chester had only won four games combined between the 1960 and 1961 seasons. The year 1963 was not much better, as they only managed a 3–6 record.

Despite a poor showing the season before, the 1963 Chester football team found itself on the opposite end of the spectrum. With losses only to Lancaster and eventual 3-AAA State Champion Gaffney, Chester finished the 1963 season with an 11–2 record and won the 1963 AA state championship. Coach Rivers could now claim two state titles as an assistant in four years of coaching.

After Chester's championship season, Rivers received a phone call. "Lancaster called me…they said that my former boss, Wade Corn, was going to take over as head coach at the newly opened Dorman High School," Rivers recalled. "Long story short, Lancaster appreciated what I had done while I was there before and offered the head coaching job." From 1964 to 1967, Rivers led Lancaster High as head coach.

When asked if it was his goal to be a head coach, Rivers said that "if it happened, it happened. I would have been just as happy as an assistant. However, yes, in my mind I knew that if the opportunity presented itself, I would take it." While at Lancaster, Rivers would boast two winning and two losing seasons with a combined record of 20–19–4. His most successful season was the 1964 season with an 8–1–2 record. Despite posting a respectable overall record at Lancaster, Rivers began to look for opportunities elsewhere.

Good Football Area

"After four seasons, and although it was great down there (Lancaster), I was becoming unhappy; Littlefield had just resigned as head coach, and I called about the position," says Rivers about his initial contact with Byrnes. Rivers elaborated by saying, "Not too much later, they called me into the district office and told me I had the job if I wanted it; and honestly, it was not a hard decision to make. I knew that Duncan was a good football area, and that they loved football in that community."

When asked if family had anything to do with his decision, Rivers said that "my wife (Barbara) had family down in Walhalla, and being in Duncan gave them a chance to be closer to the family." Dalton went on to say that his wife was "always supportive of his career and was a great coach's wife."

Social Change

Dalton Rivers is not only remembered for being one of the most successful coaches at Byrnes, he is also remembered for being the first coach at Byrnes to coach a fully integrated football team. A couple of weeks after his initial hiring, Rivers received a peculiar phone call from District 5. "They called and informed me that the school district had decided to fully desegregate (the athletic department had already begun to integrate the athletic teams) and combine with Florence Chapel and asked how would I handle integration, and when and if the students did not get along?" Rivers recalls. He says that he followed up by saying that "to desegregate the schools is a wonderful thing, and that I would handle it just like I would handle any student, be it that they are black, white…my staff and I will treat everyone with respect and as individuals…and it will all work out." While some area schools experienced high tension during this time in our country's history, by all accounts, Byrnes was blessed with a smooth transition.

Solid Foundation

Byrnes High was only twelve years old and had enjoyed a solid foundation on the field when Rivers took over. However, the 1965 through 1967 football seasons had not been a cakewalk. Joe Hazle's last season (1965) saw the Rebels finish 3–7–1. (This record is not indicative of Coach Hazle's tenure; he was a great coach for the Rebs.) In 1966 and 1967, the Rebels had only managed to win five games combined. So, to say that Dalton Rivers was under pressure was an understatement. "Before I arrived, the school had only won three games in the last season. However, when I got there, I saw the talent I had, I knew we could win...we just busted our tails and went to work," says Rivers.

Ray Johnson, no. 31, blocks for Julius McDonald, no. 32, in the 1969 game against Greer. *Courtesy of Byrnes High School.*

Obviously the hard work paid off. Rivers's first season as head coach at Byrnes laid the groundwork for things to come. Armed with players like former Florence Chapel quarterback Maddison Meadows, fullback Ray Johnson, offensive lineman Larry Cohen and linebacker Kenneth "Nappy" Johnson, Coach Rivers led Byrnes's first fully integrated team to a great finish. "We finished the '68 season 7–4, which was huge, considering they had only won three games the year before. That season was a testament to the hard work those kids had put in during the offseason," recalls Rivers. "The '68 season was a great year. Coach Rivers told us that if we did what they told us to do on the field; we could and would win. In fact, we would have made the playoffs that season; however, back then they had a coin toss when two teams tied for the same place in region, and we lost the coin toss," says Madison Meadows, Byrnes class of 1969.

First Championship

During Coach Rivers's nine seasons at Byrnes, he would only suffer one losing season (1971; 4–6–1). The Rebels would have had more appearances in the playoffs during his tenure, but back then, the SCHSL (South Carolina High School League) only allowed the top-two teams from your region into the playoffs. Despite having great team records, Rivers's Rebels only made the playoffs twice (1975 and 1976); however, the second trip would prove worthwhile.

Byrnes finished the 1976 season 12–1–1, with their only loss coming to Clinton and a tie with Woodruff, which was the Wolverines' only blemish that season. (Woodruff would go on to win the 1976 AA state title.) Byrnes dominated the 1976 playoffs, only allowing opposing teams fourteen points throughout the four-game playoff series. After twenty-one years as a school, Byrnes—led

Dalton Rivers coaches a player in 1972. *Courtesy of Byrnes High School.*

by Rivers—won its first football state championship against Bishop England by a score of 32–7.

"The '76 Championship team was by far one of the best teams I ever coached," says Rivers. He went on to say that "those guys had come up through the middle school together, played JV together and had found success at every level…and it was how much those guys cared for one another; that's only part of what made them successful." Truly, the 1976 team was loaded, and until this day, the 1976 roster is one that folks in town still talk about. On defense, they had defensive ends Bill Smith and Steve Durham and safety John McCarroll; on offense, you had quarterback Marshall Meadows and running back Mike Peake. The names listed are only a few of the greats to play on that team, as it took more than a few guys to win. To win, it took a team effort and great coaching. Rivers's overall record at Byrnes after the 1976 season was 64–33–4, including a region championship (1975) and a state championship.

From Rebel to Centurion

Following the 1976 season, Dalton Rivers left Byrnes and went to Broome. It did not take Rivers long to find success with the Centurions. In his ten seasons with Broome, Rivers guided his team to the playoffs six times and managed to lead the Centurions to the 1981 3-A state championship. Rivers's second trip to a title game as a head coach, however, did not result in a win. In that game, Myrtle Beach defeated Broome 22–6. Just as he did at his former schools, Rivers turned a fledgling program into a championship contender.

Ironically, Rivers would get the chance to play against Byrnes four times while at Broome. In those four games, Broome came out on top in all but one. His only loss against Byrnes was during the second round of the 3-A playoffs, when Byrnes, led by Bo Corne, defeated Broome 14–9 en route to the Rebels' second state championship. When Rivers left Broome after the 1986 season, his overall record was 70–41. As of 2010, his overall record at Broome is still the highest win percentage of any football head coach at the school.

Raising Beagles

Now living in Thomson, Georgia, Dalton raises hunting beagles. He says that "beagles have been a hobby of mine for quite some time, they keep me busy."

Looking Back

When asked who the biggest rival for him was while at Byrnes, Rivers says it was Greer. "In the Duncan and Greer communities, back then, everyone lived near each other; we shopped at the same stores, went to the same churches, saw each other in town. It was hard not to hear the Greer fans heckle you in town, but it was a fun rivalry," says Rivers. He followed up by saying, "Before I came to Byrnes, the Rebels had not beaten Greer in a while, so whenever we came out on top, it meant a lot to me as a coach."

Dalton still keeps up with Byrnes when he can. Just a couple of seasons ago, he came up for a home game honoring the 1976 championship team and says he has watched the Rebels from time to time on ESPN. Dalton left behind a great legacy at Byrnes. Not only is Rivers remembered for leading the Byrnes football team to their first state championship, he is also remembered fondly by former colleagues and players for being a great leader on the field, in the class and for being able to make athletes play beyond their ability.

Whether fans realize it, there is one more little-known fact about Coach Rivers: he introduced the red trim on the jerseys. Why? Rivers says that he "did it for no other reason but to 'liven' them up."

JAMES "BO" CORNE

Anyone who has attended, played or followed the Byrnes Football team in the last forty years knows Bo Corne. Twenty-four years after his 4-AAAA championship and final season, many people in our community still hold Coach Corne as the standard in coaching in District 5. To some, he is the face of Byrnes football.

Hometown Kid

Bo Corne grew up in Duncan. Like everyone else who grew up in this district, Corne received all twelve years of his primary education in District 5 and played a variety of sports growing up. While at Byrnes, Corne played Rebel baseball, junior varsity basketball, ran track and, of course, played football. His football career began at an early age, of which he says, "Like everyone else who grew up here, I played football at District 5 Junior High, which would become D.R. Hill Middle before playing at Byrnes."

While on the Rebel football team, Corne played offensive guard and linebacker. Looking back on his days as a Rebel, Corne says that he "wasn't a great athlete, but Coach (Alf) McGinnis had a profound impact on me as a coach. He made me believe that I was a great player; I wasn't a great athlete, but he could inspire people to believe they were great athletes, and that is exactly what he did for me." The Rebels were a solid team during Corne's four years. During his senior season, the Rebels finished 9–2, which at the time was the best record the Rebels had posted until that time.

Next Stop—Boone, North Carolina

Obviously, Corne was a better athlete than he gives himself credit for because his playing days went beyond those as a Rebel. Corne continued his football career at Appalachian State. He says that his route to receiving a scholarship was different than what most student-athletes experience today. Corne says that during his senior year, "Coach (Joe) Hazle, who was our head coach back then at Byrnes, took a group of us up to Appalachian State. Back then, they would hold tryouts, and they would give coaches a chance to bring in guys from their team to tryout. So, I went through the practice routine, some of the coaches had a chance to see me, and at the end of the tryouts, you went home and waited to see what happened."

When asked if he thought he would be given a chance, he said that he "didn't know. I hoped so, but I had no idea what would happen." Two weeks after the tryouts, Corne says he received a letter in the mail.

"They offered me a partial scholarship; I was excited." Corne explained that during those days, schools only gave full scholarships to one, maybe two guys on the team. However, Corne said "that the scholarship was enough money so that my parents could afford the rest."

While attending at Appalachian State, he played for Jim Duncan (1964) and Carl Messerre (1965–7). Playing offensive line, the impact that Coach McGinnis had on Corne must have carried over into his college career, as Corne was named captain his senior year. The Mountaineers fared well during his four years, placing third in the Southern Conference in 1964 and second place in 1967.

The Military Draft

During the late 1960s, many young men were drafted as a result of the Vietnam conflict. As fate would have it, Bo would be one of them. However, his story is an uncommon one. "The air force drafted me in '68 and sent me to the Lackland Air Force Base," says Corne. Shortly after being drafted, like all soldiers, Corne began basic training. A peculiar thing happened, though, as all soldiers go through a series of physical fitness tests; Corne did as well, yet something did not go as planned after basic. "I had injured my knee while playing football at Appalachian State and towards the end of my training it began to act up. So, the air force was in a dilemma in regards to my knee. They told me that if I stayed in the air force, they would not only operate on my knee, but they would also have to pay me disability for the rest of my life," says Corne. He elaborated by saying "the reason they refused to operate was because I injured my knee before I was drafted, so because it was preexisting, they did not have to." When asked if he was disappointed by the outcome, he said "not really; but I would have liked the chance to have been a pilot."

Corne says that although the air force would not pay his knee operation, it did pay the fees for one hospital bill. Which one? Corne said that "they paid for our labor and delivery bill, because before being officially discharged, my wife gave birth to our daughter."

Entering Education

After coming home unexpectedly early, Bo needed a job. Almost immediately, an old friend in District 5 helped him find a job. However, what some folks in town may not know is that the job was not in District 5 but was actually in Greenville County. "I came out of basic with the school year halfway over. Fortunately, someone helped me get a job lined up with the Greenville County School District. Greenville hired me as a P.E. coach, and I split my school day between Paris Elementary, Brushy Creek Elementary and Taylors Elementary, driving between the three schools."

While having a job in education was Corne's objective leaving college, he said that "my goal as a kid was to come back and teach and coach at Byrnes. I never entertained the thought of coaching anywhere else." As the 1968–9 school year was coming to a close, Corne was offered a job to come and teach physical education at the D.R. Hill Annex (the former WLT/Florence Chapel building) and coach football. While grateful that Greenville County gave him a job, Corne was ready—and happy—to come back home.

Back Home in Duncan

While most alumni remember Bo as "the" coach of the Rebels, it may be a surprise to realize that Corne spent the 1969–70 season as the coach of the D.R. Hill Annex Tigers. "We played some of the ninth-grade teams in the area," Corne recalls. "Not all schools had the ability to field a ninth-grade team due to student population size, and for a while after the late '60s, Byrnes would only field a J.V. and varsity." Corne's time as coach of the Tigers would be brief, as Corne would be asked by Dalton Rivers to come up to Byrnes and be an assistant with the varsity Rebels. After only a year in coaching, Corne had met his goal of coaching at Byrnes.

When asked what his first role was on the varsity coaching staff, Corne said that "I guess you could say that I called the defense; however, back then, I was not actually looked at as a defensive coordinator, but if you were to give my responsibility a title, I guess that's what it would have been."

With Dalton Rivers as the head coach and Corne as one of the assistants, the Rebels were in unfamiliar territory that season. For the 1970 and 1971 football seasons, Byrnes was moved up to 4-AAAA and assigned to Region 3. While this may be an adjustment for some teams, Byrnes had competed against larger schools in nonregion play for years. Corne's first season on varsity would prove to be a successful one, as the Rebels would finish the season with a 4–2 region record and 7–3 record overall. Another impressive statistic from the 1970 season was that Byrnes faced Gaffney for the first time and won by a score of 7–6.

In 1973, the Rebels would drop back to 3-AAA, and with two seasons under his belt on the varsity staff, Corne was earning a reputation as a determined and hardworking assistant. His tenure as the Byrnes head football coach was not far away.

1976

Entering the 1976 football season, the team knew that they were capable of having a special season. Looking back, Bo said that "the 1976 squad could be the best team to have ever played at Byrnes. Yes, there have been many great teams that have come through since, and even before then, but as far as talent across the board, they could be considered one of the best." Corne added that "even though I was just an assistant on that team, and had not become the head coach yet, that season means a lot to me." With an overall record of 12–1–1, the 1976 football team not only won the school its first state title, but it is also still a team against which later teams have been compared.

Not long after winning state, Dalton Rivers resigned as head coach. Surely, as any community would, folks in town wondered why anyone would leave after winning state. Whatever his reasons were, his departure left a job opening, and someone had to fill it. Soon after, Bo Corne was named the new head coach of the Byrnes High School football team.

Head Coach

When Bo was asked about his ambitions of being a head coach at some point in his career, he said that "I entered the profession to be a head coach; however, I never set a time line in reaching my goal. But I always wanted to be the best coach there was." Looking back on his first season as the head coach, Corne says that "we had just won a state title; we had some talent coming back, and expectations in town were at an all-time high." Corne's first season ended with a 3–6–1 record; however, the Rebels's final record was not as bleak as their record indicated. Highlights from that season would include a tie with eventual 2-A State Champion Woodruff and back-to-back shutouts over Riverside and Southside to close out the season. If the last two games were any indication of things to come for Corne and the Rebels, the outlook for 1978 was a great one.

"Looking back, that first year, I had to grow in the job. If I knew then what I know now, maybe things would have turned out differently that year, but any head coach looking back on a season may think that," says Corne. After 1977, Corne never posted another losing record. As the seasons went by, Byrnes maintained their blue-collar image as a team that could compete with anyone.

Reentering the Championship Picture

Byrnes reemerged at the championship game in 1982. With an all-star team loaded with talent, Byrnes welcomed Myrtle Beach at Nixon Field for the 3-AAA state championship. The Seahawks, coached by Doug Shaw, were attempting to win their third title in a row. Although Byrnes was hosting the championship game, by most accounts the Rebels were the underdogs. In a game that is often remembered for how muddy the field was, Byrnes and Myrtle Beach battled back and forth in a defensive showdown. A late-game field goal and a dominate defense held the Seahawks back, giving Byrnes its second state championship and Corne's first ever as a head coach.

Now it seemed that all of the knowledge that Bo Corne had learned over the years was paying off. With every win, Corne was building his legacy and establishing himself as one of the best head coaches in the state. By this time in his coaching career, Corne was on his way to becoming the head coach with the most wins in Byrnes history.

Bo would go on to lead the Rebels to back-to-back nine-win seasons and qualify for the playoffs following the 1982 championship. The 1985 season would see the Rebels return to the playoffs for the fourth-consecutive season and to the state championship game. However, this time the Rebels would be competing for their first-ever 4-AAAA Division II title against Hillcrest-Dalzell. Corne says that "the '85 team had great chemistry; they loved each other; and there was great balance on the offense and defense." Sadly, the Rebels fell short that game by a final score of 14–13.

The offseason came and went, and before long the 1986 season was upon the Rebels. Despite losing in the finals the year before, expectations were once again very high for Byrnes. Byrnes opened up the season with a shutout of rival Greer and would mount impressive wins over Big 16 foes Rock Hill, Northwestern and Dorman. The Rebels entered the 4-AAAA Division II playoffs with a dominating defense and a powerful offense. Ultimately, Corne and the Rebels found themselves back at Williams-Bryce Stadium; this time around, however, they faced the Berkeley Stags. From the opening kickoff, the Rebels never allowed the Stags to hang around, as the Rebels would bring home a third title in school history and the second for Coach Corne.

Hanging up the Whistle

After winning his second state championship as a head coach, Bo Corne must have felt great. And although the desire to come back the next season may have been strong, Corne decided to retire from coaching. "After talking it over with my wife and looking back on what I had managed to do with the program, I decided to step down as head coach," says Corne. Corne also said that he "entered the profession to be a head coach. My dream and goal was to win state." Remarkably, Corne had accomplished his goal. Not only did Corne surpass Dalton Rivers in state championships won at Byrnes, but he also eclipsed Rivers's overall win mark at Byrnes.

Bo Corne would step to the front office during the next season and become an assistant principal at the high school. Despite no longer having a presence on the field the next few years, students would still refer to him as "Coach." After thirty wonderful years in education, Bo Corne retired from District 5 schools in January 1999. After retirement, Corne took on a new assignment: working for Horace Mann. As of this printing, Corne is still member of the publicly elected school board in District 5.

The Red Star

Anyone who has played as a Rebel knows what the "red star" means to the football program. There has been some speculation about the red star for years, wondering who established the tradition. Coach Corne finally revealed the story behind it.

So, what's the deal with the stars? Corne answered by saying, "I was intrigued with the Dallas Cowboys. You know, they were referred to as America's Team because they were the best, and everyone knew about the stars on their helmets and jerseys; those stars really stood out. At the same time, we were one of the best teams in the state, and at the same time, some of the players had been pushing us to put some red color into our jerseys. So, after the '82 season, we were ordering some new jerseys, and there happened to be enough space to fit a star on each side of (of the word Byrnes) the jersey. Well, we stuck those stars on there and made them red."

Corne later added that "those stars stood out. Those red stars were intended to represent the players and groups that had came through before; and furthermore, those red stars were intended to remind younger players about the guys before them that had worked hard to earn that stars, and I am glad that Bobby (Bentley) chose to continue that tradition."

Leaving a Legacy

When asked what it was like to be the head coach at Byrnes, Corne said that "it's not just a job, it's a responsibility to the community. In Duncan, mediocrity is not acceptable. This town wants to be the best...and not just in football. Look at the band, look at the recent success the baseball team and football team; the town wants to be the best." Corne later added that "I am proud that most of the players and athletes were better than when I played. I cared about all of those kids...I just wanted them to play better than they could have believed."

Corne is still a prominent figure in the community, and he can be found at nearly every Byrnes football game and often times at the games of the Lady Rebels softball team, for whom his granddaughter plays. "Hey, I am the biggest fan Byrnes has got," Corne said.

BOBBY BENTLEY

Like Bo Corne, Bobby Bentley is a hometown guy who grew up in the same community in which he played and coached. Winning a state championship is a goal of most head coaches; winning four state championships in a row is something of which most head coaches can only dream. Coach Bentley managed to do both. Only two other football programs (Woodruff 1975–8 and Florence 1916–9) and one other coach (W.L. Varner) can claim this honor. Bentley's rise through the Byrnes ranks is one that most hometown guys would love to accomplish.

Rebels

Bobby Bentley, a multisport athlete while at Byrnes, began playing football for the Rebels in 1983. "Coach Tommy Woodward saw me throwing around the gym my freshman year and asked me to come out and see how I liked football; so, I came out that summer," says

Bentley. While at Byrnes, Bentley is usually remembered by most as quarterback, but he also played at corner on the defense. Bentley's time as a Rebel was one of the most memorable times at Byrnes, as the Rebels finished 9–3 in both 1983 and 1984 and ultimately made it back to the state championship in 1985.

"My senior year was memorable for me. I was given the chance to be the starter (at QB); our opening game was against Greer, which we won; and then we beat Dorman that year," says Bentley. Truly, the Rebels had a fine season that year, as they would only lose three regular season games. Byrnes would go on and cruise into the playoffs, dominating Union, Brookland-Cayce and Airport. When the smoke cleared, Byrnes and Hillcrest-Dalzell were the only ones still standing. In a game that went back and forth, dominated by defense from both teams, Hillcrest-Dalzell managed to stop the Rebels by a score of 14–13. Despite not winning state that year, Bentley's performance as quarterback that season is still talked about today, and because of his abilities, he was able to garner the attention of college recruiters. Bentley concluded his high school career as a quarterback for the North team in the 1985 North-South All-Star Football game.

Blue Hose

With Bobby Bentley's career as a Rebel coming to a conclusion, it was time for him to decide where to go next. With a handful of colleges showing him some attention, Bentley picked Presbyterian College. When asked why, Bentley said that "they were a good fit. I liked the staff down there." For his freshman season, Bentley was redshirted. His sophomore year, Bentley was once again taking snaps as a quarterback for Presbyterian College. Bentley wrapped up his playing career as a free safety for the Blue Hose during his junior and senior years. When all was said and done, Presbyterian College had an impressive team while Bentley was there, as they always fielded competitive teams in the South Atlantic Conference.

As Bentley's career at the college was wrapping up, it was time to start thinking about post-college plans. In a matter of good timing,

Presbyterian College's defensive coordinator, Bruce Hill, had just taken a head coaching job with a local high school in the Upstate. Hill asked Bentley to come with him, to which Bentley agreed. However, some Rebel faithful may be surprised where Bentley ended up.

Bulldogs?

In 1990, just four years after graduating from Byrnes, Bobby Bentley found himself coaching. In one of the biggest "what could have been?" situations in Duncan, Bentley's first coaching job was not at Byrnes, but at Boiling Springs High School. "Coach Hill had just taken the head coaching job at Boling Springs, and he asked me if I would come and coach for him, and I accepted," reveals Bentley. Bentley added that "I worked at their spring practice, and shortly into the summer; however, Boiling Springs never gave me a teaching contract." As summer practice was getting started at area high schools, Bentley received a phone call from longtime District 5 employee Harold McManus. "Coach McManus called me and said that there was a contract waiting on me at Byrnes. Coach Hill asked me to stay, but like I said, there was no contract," said Bentley. So, after almost becoming a coach on the Bulldogs staff, Bobby Bentley was coming home to Duncan.

Back Home

With summer practice underway for the 1990 season, Bentley found himself right back in the loop with second-year head coach Fred Coan. "I started out coaching DBs and QBs," says Bentley.

Those early years on the varsity staff was a tough period for the Rebels and Bentley, as some of the pride and tradition of the '70s and '80s had worn off. A couple of seasons before Bentley returned, Byrnes was dropped back to 3-AAA, which, for the most part, they had managed to make a smooth transition. Byrnes would finish out their time in 3-AAA at the end of the 1991 season and begin

4-AAAA competition at the beginning of the 1992 season. Despite a less-than-stellar finish in 1992, Byrnes would manage to win the Region 1 4-AAAA Championship and would qualify for the playoffs.

The year 1994 once again proved to be a good year for the Rebels, as they would place second in the region and once again qualify for the playoffs. When asked if he looked at things differently in 1994 as he did in 1990, Bentley said, "I learned about building a relationship with the kids, that it wasn't just about the Xs and Os." While Byrnes was rebuilding under Coach Coan, Bentley was putting in extra work and effort, which was about to pay off.

At the conclusion of the 1994 season, Coach Coan approached Bentley. "Coach Coan told me that McManus was going to retire as AD and asked if I would like to be head coach. I had always wanted to be a head coach; I wanted to be like Bo Corne, and I knew that I had wanted to be a head coach by the time I was thirty, but here it was—this chance was coming a lot sooner than I had planned," recalls Bentley. In the winter of 1995, Bobby Bentley was named the ninth head coach of Byrnes High School and the third alumnus of Byrnes to be named head coach.

Head Coach

Becoming a head coach can be stressful. However, it can become even more stressful when you are also the youngest 4-AAAA head coach in the state and when you have assistants on your staff who are twice your age. When asked about some of his concerns and goals, Bentley responded by saying that "I was thinking about the older guys, whether or not they would follow me. Also, I wanted to build back the tradition that had been lost, reminding guys of what it was like before, and I was also determined to get more players on the team."

Bentley's first season at the helm was a challenge, not just for the team, but for him, too. "It was a complete struggle. My staff and I were facing resistance from both parents and players; some players did not buy in to what we were doing; it was tough." The Rebels would close out the 1995 season with a 2–9 record. The year 1996 did not go much better as the Rebels would finish 1–10. Despite a rough start in a young career, Bentley remained optimistic and committed to leading the Rebels in the right direction.

Breakout Game

With only three wins under his belt, Bobby Bentley remained committed to his players. With offseason workouts and a squad of players who believed in the offense, there was change in the air. "The players believed in the system; they were committing to the offseason workouts and trying to make themselves better," says Bentley. The 1997 season started off with a bang as the Rebels defeated Eastside 31–7. Byrnes would win its first four games that season, including an impressive win over rival Greer, 42–27. Despite dropping a few losses, this was a reenergized Rebels squad—a team that believed no one could beat them. The next game on the Byrnes schedule was a game that showed a glimpse of things to come.

With a 5–3 record, Bentley and the Rebels marched into Gibbs Stadium for a showdown with the three-time defending Big 16 state champions, Spartanburg. The Vikings had only lost to Byrnes one time (1990) since 1976, so by all accounts, the Rebels were the underdogs. With much hype and little respect for the Rebels, Byrnes defeated Spartanburg 31–25. Media outlets all over the state named that game the biggest upset of the season. Bentley says "that was the breakout game that was proof that the players believed in the system." Byrnes would close out the 1997 season with an 8–5 record and its first playoff victory since 1986.

With a phenomenal season behind them, the Rebels entered the offseason with a lot of confidence. At the beginning of the 1998 season, expectations were high for the Rebels. Once again, the Rebels won their first four contests of the season; however, no team in Byrnes history had won by such large margins. Byrnes defeated Eastside 68–22, Greer 52–3, Mauldin 70–6 and T.L. Hanna 65–6. Truly, Bentley had created one of the most explosive offenses in school history. Byrnes's only losses that season came to much larger, Big 16 schools that had much more depth. Byrnes entered the 1998 playoffs as an overwhelming favorite among local newspapers as a state title competitor. In a rematch of the 1986 championship game, Byrnes welcomed Berkley to Nixon Field and won 49–14. For the second round, Byrnes faced Ridgeview. In a defensive showdown, Ridgeview upset the heavily favored Byrnes. Byrnes finished the 1998 season with a 7–6 record that, by most accounts, does not represent how good Bentley's team was that year.

Bringing Back Tradition

Bobby Bentley would only have one more losing season (1999) as head coach at Byrnes. With the 2000 season, Byrnes would not only be primed for becoming one of the best programs in school history, but they were on their way to becoming the most dominant team in state history. "Once (Mike) Srock came on board, I could focus on other aspects of the team. Srock was always there. Now I had eyes in the weight room at all times; now we could do workouts year-round with someone we could trust; and someone that really cared about the strength program," Bentley says when asked about one of the keys to the team getting better. Obviously, all of the offseason programs and commitments from the players were paying off.

The 2000 season proved to be a successful one, as the Rebels would finish the season with an 8–5 record and impressive wins over Spartanburg and Gaffney. As good as 2000 was, 2001 was the year that the Rebels would begin an amazing streak. For instance, since 2001 the Rebels have made it to the third round or beyond in every season except one (2006). When asked if he knew how good the Rebels were poised to be, Bentley said, "After 2000, I knew there were players there to back us up; I knew we would be good…I had no idea about the national success to come, but I knew that success was there and ready to go." Bentley added that "around this time, some of the best years of my life were happening. The kids liked us as a staff. There was love—the players felt it—and no one was questioning us and what we were doing. Really, the biggest difference between 2000–2006 when compared to 1995–1999 was the response the players had with the coaching."

In a season that saw victories over Gaffney and Rock Hill and one-point losses to Spartanburg and Dorman, Byrnes broke through in 2001. Finally, for the first time since 1986, the Rebels made it to the third round of the state playoffs. That third round is still talked about today, as it is remembered for its pouring rain and a late game-winning touchdown that gave Conway its win. Yet, despite their loss, Bentley and the Rebels had finally brought back the tradition at Byrnes—a tradition of winning and being one of the most dominant teams in the state.

1, 2, 3, 4 in a Row

When asked what the difference maker was in his coaching philosophy, he said, "Looking back, some of the things I was doing at the time all makes sense. I started treating the players like they were my kids, and not just like my players, and I began to let coaching be what I did, not who I was. A lot of that I owe to my wife, Paulette, who I started dating around July of 2000. She helped me tie up the loose ends in my life, got some things in order in regards to my faith and the things I was doing off the field. She brought stability to my life, which had a direct impact with things I was doing on the field and off."

Coming off their heartbreaking loss to Conway, Bentley and the Rebels set out to do something that had not been done in years: win a football state championship. The year 2002 brought about a new era for Byrnes. Byrnes entered the 2002 playoffs with a 10–1 record, with the only loss coming against Evangel Christian of Louisiana. Battling through the playoffs, Byrnes dominated their opponents. Finally, after sixteen years, the Rebels found themselves in the 4-AAAA Division II finals. Their opponent: Conway. Despite losing to Conway the year before, Byrnes was not concerned with revenge. Conway was just another opponent in the Rebels' way. After dominating Conway in the first half, Byrnes held off a Tigers rally in the fourth quarter to guarantee its first state championship in sixteen years. Byrnes, winning by a score of 34–28, was once again the 4-AAAA Division II champion.

Bentley and the Rebels' success would not be limited to one state title. Byrnes would follow up the 2002 title by winning the next three. Byrnes would finish 15–0 in 2003 and would once again meet Conway in the finals; however, this time the final score would be much more one-sided, as the Rebels won 40–14. Not only had Byrnes won two titles back to back, but the 15–0 mark would also be the first undefeated season in the football team's history. Byrnes went on to win two more titles in row, with the last two titles being won against Irmo (2004) and Richland Northeast (2005). Byrnes's record during this span was an amazing 57–2.

Many players' names became synonymous with Byrnes football during the 2002–5 run. When asked which player stood out the most during the championship run, Bentley answered by saying "there are so many great memories during that time, it's hard to single anyone out; everyone had their part." Just as Bentley had said before, his goal was to bring back the tradition that former head coaches had established, and with obvious results, he had met his goal. Not only had Bentley reestablished the tradition in Rebel football, but he also managed to surpass the championship totals of a coach he had looked up to since he was in the fourth grade, which was none other than Bo Corne.

Saying Goodbye

Byrnes opened up the 2006 season with high expectations. Hoping to win an unprecedented fifth title in a row, hardly anyone believed the Rebels would not repeat. Despite having a great season, the Rebels would fall short in their quest. Byrnes would close out the season with an impressive 11–2 record. What happened at the conclusion of the season was something that shocked the state. Shortly after the 2006 season ended, Coach Bentley announced that he would be stepping down as the head coach of the Rebels and would immediately take over as the newly named head coach of the Presbyterian College football team. The entire community was stunned; however, most everyone knew that after becoming one of the most successful coaches in the state, the time was coming when

Bentley would take over a college program. Bentley would leave Byrnes as the football coach with the most wins in school history. His record was 107–52 at Byrnes.

Blue Hose

Bobby Bentley returned to Presbyterian College, after the 2006 football season, as the head football coach. This was the second time in his career he was able to lead a team he once played for. When asked about his decision, he simply said, "I wanted something different, a challenge. Plus it was a great opportunity, and I was able to keep the kids at home (in Lyman)." The college was at a crossroads when Bentley came in, as it was beginning the process of moving up to the NCAA Division I. Bentley was met with great success his rookie year leading the Blue Hose. In 2007, Presbyterian College finished 6–5, with a monstrous road schedule and only three home games. Not only would Bentley guide the Blue Hose to a successful inaugural year in Division I, but his team would also go on to break several NCAA offensive football records.

After two seasons with the college, Bentley decided that his time there was coming to an end. Bentley would leave Presbyterian College in January 2009. While his time at the college was short, it was a memorable and successful one.

Down the Road and Back Again

Following his departure from Presbyterian College, District 5 announced that Bobby Bentley was returning home. However, this time, his role would be different. Currently, Bentley is the public relations representative and the districtwide athletic director. When asked about his return and his new job, Bentley said that "it felt good coming home. This time though, I get to work with all of the principals, which is new for me. I had only been an AD for half a year before I left last time, so this new role is exciting for me." Bentley added that "my goal is to do for the other sports what we did for football."

Aside from his districtwide athletic director job and his public relations position, Bentley is currently the associate head football coach and the offensive coordinator.

When asked if there is something that he has taken away from during his years as a coach, he says that "you don't always see the details of the big picture as a young coach, but you can train yourself to be a better leader."

CHRIS MILLER

Paris Mountain

Growing up in a state park provides a lot of opportunities to stay busy and active. Chris Miller was able to live this life since his father, Ed Miller, was the superintendent of Paris Mountain State Park in Greenville. According to Miller, this lifestyle helped define who he was, not only as a person, but also as an athlete. "There was always something going on up there. For instance, almost every weekend, there would be some sort of game going on up there. See, the park had a football field and a baseball field, and usually I would wander up there and stand around and watch until someone noticed me. After a while, the guys would call over to me and ask me to play. Those fields are where I got a lot of my desire to play (sports). I always tried to get in on a game on Sundays and Saturdays," says Miller. Miller also said that "the park offered a lot of ways to stay fit, and one of the things I used to do was I would go off and run through the woods, imagining the trees as other players; I would cut through them, weave in and out, in a way, imagining I was competing against other guys."

Because Miller grew up in Greenville, he played for a couple of the local recreation leagues. "I started playing football when I was ten for the Ballenger Bulldozers." The very next year, Miller began playing for his brother, Ed Jr., and Larry Pace on the Brookwood Forest Rams. "Many coaches made an impact on me, but my brother Ed Jr.—he probably had the biggest impact on me when I was a player." From the time he was eleven until he was fourteen,

Miller was on Brookwood's team. Usually, kids start playing for their local high school at fourteen; however, Miller said that "my brother kept me with him until he thought I was ready to play for the high school, and that's how it was growing up, my brothers, Ed and Bobby, had taught me about football growing up." The Rams only lost two games during Miller's time with the team.

Living the Dream

"Growing up, my dream was to be a (Wade Hampton) General. Back then, when I was a kid, they had a great team; and at the time, there was no Eastside, Riverside High Schools; on my side of town, the only school was Wade Hampton. I was bound and determined to play for Wade Hampton," says Miller. While at Wade Hampton, Miller played for longtime head coach Bill Phillips. Miller must have made an immediate impact upon his arrival, as he was named a starter on the Generals' defense.

"Just as my brother had an impact on me as a player, John Carlisle and Mike Hawkins were big influences for me not only as a player and coaching style, but as a person as well," responded Miller when asked about some of his positive influences from Wade Hampton. Position-wise, it should come as no surprise that Miller could be found on the defensive side of the ball as a linebacker. However, it may come as a surprise that Miller had always been a backup at quarterback as well. "My senior year I started as QB, and although I was a defensive player, I had to do it for the team. I had fun playing as QB, though," Miller said.

Despite not having a stellar overall record, Wade Hampton was always a competitive football team during Miller's years. When asked about his most memorable season, Miller said that "our senior year, we went 5–6. We were a very talented team, very good, but we never could win the 'big game.' We were a team that was on the move—really stepping up—because our guys, those seniors had never really won any big games. But my senior class, we were good; had we managed to get that big win, we could have went a lot further that year." Miller would end his high school playing career by playing in the 1975 Shrine Bowl and the 1975 North-South All-Star game.

Although Wade Hampton had not gone as far as he may have hoped, Miller was gaining the attention of college recruiters. Miller was receiving offers from Catawba, Newberry, the Citadel and Gardner-Webb, to name a few. In the end, Miller chose to continue his playing career as a Newberry Indian.

Newberry

When asked about his decision on attending Newberry College, Miller said, "I chose Newberry for a couple of reasons. For one, not all of the offers were full rides; and although my parents made a great living and always provided us with everything we needed, Newberry offered the most, and that's part of the reason I took it was to help my family."

While at Newberry, Miller would stand out as a playmaker on the defense, and just as he had coaches before college make an impact on him, Miller once again found himself playing for great ones. "Coach Cumby stands out in my mind; he was a real fiery guy. He was always trying to motivate us, and he was so knowledgeable. There are some things that I still do now as a coach that I learned from him," says Miller about his former position coach.

Miller's four seasons with the Indians were memorable ones. While Miller was at Newberry, the Indians—who competed in the NAIA during that time—at one point were ranked as high as seventh in the country and managed to win the fabled "Bronze Derby" from the Presbyterian College Blue Hose. When asked about his time at Newberry, Miller said that "I would never take anything back from Newberry; I loved it. It's a great school, and one of the things that I am proud of in being an alumnus of Newberry is that they are known for putting out great coaches." Miller added that "something I believe is that every kid needs to go to school, whether or not they are playing a sport; every kid needs to go and receive the experience that comes with attending college."

Miller says that "while playing at Newberry, I knew I wouldn't be a part of the game anymore, and I knew I had to stay with it. I started to think about trying to make an impact on young guys' lives just as some of my old coaches had done for me."

Rebels

Chris Miller, as most folks in Duncan already know, began his career in education and coaching at Byrnes. When asked if he had tried to go back to his old high school, Miller said that "yes, and I had wanted to go back to Wade Hampton, but they did not have a job." So, what led him to Byrnes? Miller answers, "Well, an in-law of mine, Sandra Hadden, knew of a job opening. So, a call was made, and I applied. Just like that, they offered me a job in ISS and money to coach. I was happy to be at Byrnes."

Miller's initial time with the Rebels is a time that many fans consider to be some of the Rebels' best years. Bo Corne, by 1982, had built the Rebels into one of the most dominant teams in the state, and Miller's inclusion on the defensive side of coaching seemed to fit Bo's vision of the team. While at Byrnes, Miller would see the Rebels post solid records every season, finishing 5–4–1 (1981), 12–2 (1982), 9–3 (1983–4), 10–4 (1985) and 11–3 (1986). In his first six seasons as an assistant, Miller would be part of two state championship teams and would see the championship game three times. From the beginning, Miller was already used to seeing success while coaching.

When asked if he has carried anything with him throughout his career from that time period, Miller said that "'til this day, I have tried to have a staff like the coaching staff from back then ('82–'86). Because, as a group back then, those guys really cared about the kids; and even today, when I interview guys for my staff now, I try to find out if they agree that it's not always about the Xs and the Os, but the fact that it's about the kids." Miller decided to leave Byrnes following the 1986 season. When asked why he left, Miller answered by saying, "I was disappointed when Bo (Corne) got out of coaching, and with Bo stepping down, another opportunity presented itself." That opportunity was at Broome. "Just as Bo had given me a chance, at the time I had the chance to work with another coaching great, Jim Few, who had coached at Greer for many years. I looked at the move as a chance to move up and get more experience," said Miller.

From Royal and Gray to Royal and Gold

With the same motivation and desire that he had as an assistant at Byrnes, Miller arrived at Broome to help out with the defense. Miller's hard work and knowledge of the game took him far, as he would be offered the head coaching position at Broome after the 1991 season. When asked about the events leading to his hiring, Miller said, "I was at the right place at the right time. After spending five seasons as an assistant, Coach Few thought I was ready."

As Broome's new head coach, Miller made an immediate impact. Although Broome finished 4–7 that season, because of a late-season drive, the Centurions qualified for the 1992 playoffs. This was an accomplishment, given the fact that Broome had not been to the playoffs since the 1988 season. The next three seasons would be even better for Miller's Centurions, as they would win their region championship in 1993, 1994 and 1995 and gain playoff victories in those seasons as well. Some of the notable wins during that run included victories against 3-A powerhouse Greer, as well as some wins against much larger 4-A schools. Win asked about his favorite season at Broome, Miller said that "it would have to be the '93 season. It was my first region title, and we made it into the second round of the playoffs."

With an overall record of 36–32, with three region titles and six playoff appearances, Miller's time at Broome had been a successful one. Miller's next stop would once again grant him the chance to work with another legendary coach.

Spartanburg

Chris Miller would find himself at another Spartanburg County school, this time though it was with the Spartanburg Vikings. When asked how he ended up with Spartanburg, Miller stated, "I looked in the area, and I was offered a position at Spartan High. I looked at the chance as another way to add to my experience. I had worked with Corne, Few and now I was getting a chance to work with Doc Davis." At the time, Spartanburg was a championship contender year in and year out. Spartanburg had won four Big 16 championships under Davis during the first half of the '90s, and despite making several playoff drives every year thereafter, the Vikings had not managed to win another title since 1996.

Miller's time with Spartanburg was time well spent, and during his fourth year as an assistant, Spartanburg won its sixth state championship. Meanwhile, as it turns out, a longtime friend at Byrnes had been staying in touch with Miller over the years. "I had kept in touch with Bobby (Bentley). He would call me, even back when he became head coach; he had kept in touch with me over the years. Finally, a job came open and the timing was right," says Miller. After eighteen years, Miller was coming back to Byrnes.

Back in Duncan

When Miller was asked about how he felt returning to Byrnes, he said that "I was excited. Yet, at the same time I was a little worried about my family, because, for example, my little girl (Brayden) had grown up in Cowpens. She did not want to leave because all she had known was on that side of town. But she came through, and now she is a Blue and Gray Rebel, through and through. Cam, my son, had an easy adjustment." With Miller also came stellar defensive coaching. Prior to Miller's return, Byrnes had won back-to-back state championships, so hopes were at an all-time high in Duncan. Fans were glad to see Miller return to the school where his career began.

Miller, upon his return, brought back an old nickname from the '80s. Bobby Bentley had already been bringing back some old traditions to the football team, and he asked Miller to bring back another one. "Back in the '80s, the Rebels defense had a nickname; they were called the 'Strike Force.' Bobby told me when I came back that he wanted to bring that name back. But, they had to earn it," said Miller. Sure enough, halfway through the 2004 season, the Byrnes defense had earned that distinction and was being called the Strike Force.

With Miller calling the defense and Bentley calling the offense, Byrnes would go on to win two more state championships in a row (2004, 2005), becoming the first school to ever win four 4-AAAA Division II state championships in a row (2002–5).

After the 2006 season, the people of District 5 were shocked when they heard the news of Bobby Bentley leaving. Immediately, fans began to wonder: who would be the next head coach? "When Bobby left, the staff was sitting there, and we felt the same way we did back when Bo left in the '80s. We wanted everything to stay the same and keep the success and the drive going," Miller said. Fans and coaches alike had a reason to be concerned because the same situation presented itself back in 1986 after Corne's departure. Just like the 1986 team, hopes were high for the Rebels, and the last thing the community wanted was for a coach to come in and completely change the system, as the coach who took Corne's spot had done. With a huge sigh of relief, the community was excited to hear that Bentley's replacement would come from within the staff and would be none other than Chris Miller.

Head Coach

Did Chris Miller have any hesitations in stepping up and becoming a head coach again? According to Miller, absolutely not; he was ready. The 2006 season saw the departure of many Division I signees, and some pundits across the state said that 2007 would be a rebuilding year for the Rebels. However, the only thing that was rebuilding was another run at a championship. The theme for 2007 was "A new run has begun," and with a young team full of sophomores and juniors, Miller led the Rebels to a 15–0 finish. Many young Rebels stepped up that year, including Chas Dodd, Marcus Lattimore, Nick

Marcus Lattimore on the run. *Courtesy of Pam Dunlap.*

Jones and a host of many great athletes who were ready to bring the championship back home to Duncan. Byrnes wasted no time in reclaiming its spot in Columbia. Notable wins that year include not one but two wins over rival Dorman; a huge win over the team that had eliminated Byrnes from the 2006 playoffs, Gaffney; and of course, the Rebels topped off their championship run against legendary coach John McKissick and the Summerville Greenwave. Not only had Miller and the Rebels lived up to their 2007 theme, but they had also reassured the community that the success and tradition built over the last decade was here to stay. With the 2007 title, Miller had become the first coach at Byrnes to win a state title in his first season as head coach.

Miller and the Rebels only lost one regular season game in 2008, and it was against the Dorman Cavaliers. Despite the loss, Byrnes would get its chance at redemption as they had to travel back to Dorman in the third round of the playoffs. What was the end result? Byrnes would shutdown Dorman's running game and would advance to the state finals for the sixth time in seven years. Byrnes closed out the 2008 season once again as state champions; this time though, victory came against the Sumter Gamecocks.

Miller's third year as head coach would prove to be successful one. They would finish the 2009 season as upper state champions and a final record of 13–2.

Looking back on his career, Chris Miller acknowledges how much family has meant to him. "Gina, my wife—I could never have done all of this without her. Coaching keeps you away sometimes, and it takes a special kind of woman to do the things she has done for me, not just being a wife, but in being a mother to our kids. My family has helped me in many ways because in coaching, and in life, there are many ups and down. Especially in the past year, which has been an emotional one with my hip surgery, the loss at state—without her, I could not have gotten though it all as easy," says Miller. When asked about his thoughts on what he has done for current and former players, Miller says, "Maybe they will remember me later, and maybe I was able to help them in some way, on the field or off."

As of this printing, Miller has once again led the Rebels to an appearance in the 4-AAAA Division I playoffs.

CHAPTER 5

OLD FOES AND NEW FOES

THE RIVALRIES

No one really knows exactly how rivalries are formed. Over the years, facts evolve into myth, and the myth becomes legend. Byrnes has had its share of rivalries over the years. Some are brief and come only at certain times, such as Conway during the 2001 through 2003 playoffs. But some are longstanding and have deep roots. The teams below are squads that, no matter how your season ends, the season is more successful with a win against the old rivals.

Greer Yellow Jackets
Record against Greer: 27–26–1
First Game: 1955, 60–12 (Loss)

Greer is considered Byrnes's no. 1 rival of all time. Recently, the rivalry seems to have lost its steam. Although the Rebels overtook the lead in the all-time series in 2009, for years Greer had the upper hand.

Excluding 1975, Byrnes and Greer have played every season.

The 2009 season brought a temporary halt to the series. For the near future, Greer has dropped Byrnes from their schedule. Byrnes won their last meeting 52–6.

Dorman Cavaliers
Record against Dorman: 28–27–3 (Includes Fairforest Wins/Losses)
First Game: 1955, 19–13 (Win)

The Byrnes-Dorman rivalry dates back to the days of Duncan High. Byrnes has played Dorman more than any other team.

Being so close to Byrnes, with neighborhoods running along the District 5 and 6 lines, the Dorman game has always been a featured game during the season. Within recent years, the series have become more heated, as can be seen with Byrnes and Dorman each costing the other a state championship.

Gaffney Indians
Record against Gaffney: 9–11
First Game: 1970, 7–6 (Win)

Gaffney had never been on the Rebels' schedule until we were put into Region II 4-AAAA.

The Indians have had the Rebels in their crosshairs since the beginning of the decade. Both teams have upset the other numerous times since and even cost each other a couple of region titles.

Since leaving Region II 4-AAAA in 2007, Byrnes and Gaffney have remained on each other's schedule. The rivalry came to a boiling point in 2006 when Gaffney upset the Rebels in the second round of the playoffs, stopping Byrnes on their way to a fifth-straight state championship. The Rebs would get their revenge the following season, winning 49–14.

CROSSING THE BORDER: OUT-OF-STATE RIVALS

Since 2002, the Rebels have become a national powerhouse. What started as an endeavor to get the team ready for a rigorous Region II 4-AAAA schedule, the out-of-state contests are now an expected part of the Rebels' schedule.

It's through these games that millions of eyes are on our community. Below is a quick glance at the teams Byrnes has faced, and a little history on the teams themselves.

Evangel Christian Eagles
Shreveport, Louisiana
Colors: Red, White and Blue
Louisiana State Championships: Ten
Location, Date and Result: Evangel Christian High School;
September 20, 2002; Evangel Won 21–10

Byrnes lost its first out-of-state contest in a valiant effort. Evangel— the defending 2001 Louisiana 5-A state champion—trailed Byrnes late in game. With a fourth-quarter rally, the Eagles were able to pull ahead and win the contest 21–10.

That year, Byrnes finished its season 14–1 as the 4-AAAA Division II state champions. Evangel Christian's record mirrored ours, with a 14–1 record and as Louisiana's 5A state champions.

Montgomery Bell Academy Big Red
Nashville, Tennessee
Colors: Cardinal and Silver
Tennessee State Championships: Fourteen
Location, Date and Result: Vanderbilt Stadium in Nashville,
Tennessee; August 20, 2005; Byrnes won 62–14.

At Vanderbilt Stadium, Byrnes trounced MBA 62–14. The Big Red were never really in the game, as Byrnes scored at will and often. This win was the first en route to a fourth state title in a row for the Rebels.

Byrnes finished the season with a 15–0 record.

Montgomery Bell Academy finished the 2005 season with a record of 8–3.

Glades Central Raiders
Belle Glade, Florida
Colors: Maroon and Gold
Florida State Championships: Six
Location, Date and Result: Byrnes High School;
August 26, 2006; Byrnes Won 27–15

The Rebels hit "primetime" when traditional Florida powerhouse Glades Central came to Nixon Field. Not only did this game mark the first time an out-of-state opponent would come to Byrnes, but August 26, 2006, was also the first Byrnes game to be broadcast on ESPN.

Fans from across the state packed the stadium that day. And with a noon kickoff on a Saturday and a sweltering ninety-five-plus temperature reading, fans were at a fever pitch.

Spectators across the nation witnessed the Rebels thump the Raiders 27–15 in the first of two out-of-state contests during 2006. One game at a time, Byrnes was making its presence known on the national stage.

Byrnes finished the 2006 season with a 11–2 record. They lost in the second round of the 4-AAAA Division I playoffs to Gaffney, 16–13. Glades Central finished 12–3, losing in the fourth round of the Florida 3-AAA playoffs.

Arch Bishop Moeller High School Fighting Crusaders
Cincinnati, Ohio
Colors: Blue and Gold
Ohio State Championships: Seven
Location, Date and Result: University of Cincinnati's Nippert
Stadium; September 16, 2006; Byrnes Won 21–20

Despite performing above and beyond in out-of-state competition, the Rebels still had critics saying that "Byrnes can't compete with Ohio and Florida teams." In 2006, Byrnes had already thumped a team from Florida; now it was time to face the Ohio powerhouse Moeller.

The game was part of the "Kirk Herbstreit: Ohio vs. USA Challenge," which pitted the best teams around the country against Ohio's best. The game was very tense from the beginning, with Moeller leading for almost the entire game. Thanks to a staunch defense and a powerful offense, Byrnes was able to narrowly pull off the win with a final score of 21–20.

Moeller finished 2006 with a record of 5–5.

Dr. Phillips High School Panthers
Orlando, Florida
Colors: Dark Blue and Light Blue
Florida State Championships: Zero
Location, Date and Result: Byrnes High School; September 6, 2007; Byrnes Won 18–14

With a new head coach and a team full of sophomores, Byrnes had a scare in the first half of this game. But, as the final seconds ticked away in the second half, it was clear Byrnes would keep its home winning streak alive and score a win over another out-of-state team.

Byrnes would finish 2007 with a 15–0 record as the 4-AAAA Division I state champions. Dr. Phillips, that season, had a 7–5 record and lost in the second round of Florida's 5-AAAAA state playoffs.

Centerville High School Elks
Centerville, Ohio
Colors: Red, White and Blue
Ohio State Championships: Zero
Location, Date and Result: Centerville High School; September 14, 2007; Byrnes Won 38–31 (OT)

Leading for most of the game, Byrnes found itself tied with Centerville as the final seconds ticked down in the fourth quarter. In overtime, the Rebels struck first and managed to shut down

Centerville's offense en route to their first overtime win against an out-of-state team. Byrnes sits 2–0 against Ohio teams.

Centerville, in 2007, had a 9–3 record and lost in the second round of the Ohio Division I playoffs.

North Gwinnett Bulldogs
Suwannee, Georgia
Colors: Black and Red
Georgia State Championships: Zero
Location, Date and Result: North Gwinnett High School;
August 29, 2008; Byrnes Won 36–21

Coming into the game ranked no. 1 in the nation, Byrnes had a stiff challenge in North Gwinnett. Throughout the summer of 2008, North Gwinnett and Byrnes faced each other in the Hoover 7-on-7 Passing Tournament and at the Palmetto State Showdown 7-on-7 Tournament. Needless to say, a rivalry had begun to spark before the game even took place.

Everything came to a head when the Rebels faced the Bulldogs on national television. To add hype to the game, North Gwinnett debuted solid black jerseys for a "black out," while the Rebels wore silver on silver jerseys. From the onset of the game, Gwinnett was aggressive, taking a 14–9 lead at halftime. The Rebels, however, came alive and scored 20 unanswered points to take a 29–14 lead. As the final buzzer went off, the Rebs prevailed 36–21.

In 2008, Byrnes finished the season with a 14–1 record and its second-straight 4-AAAA Division I state championship. North Gwinnett had a 10–3 record and lost in the third round of the Georgia 5-AAAAA state playoffs.

Old Foes and New Foes

Lincoln High School Trojans
Tallahassee, Florida
Colors: Green and Gold
Florida State Championships: Two
Location, Date and Result: Byrnes High School; September 19,
2008; Byrnes Won 38–0

Lincoln, Byrnes's third opponent from the Sunshine State, came to Duncan hoping to stop Byrnes's winning streak against Florida teams. Unfortunately for them, that did not happen. Byrnes won 38–0.

Lincoln ended its 2008 season with an 11–4 record as Florida's 4-AAAA state runner-up.

Pahokee High School Blue Devils
Pahokee, Florida
Colors: Red, White and Blue
Florida State Championships: Five
Location, Date and Result: Byrnes High School; October 3,
2008; Byrnes Won 38–12

A week before the game, standout linebacker Norman Griffith was murdered. In an act of courage, the Pahokee Blue Devils made the journey to Duncan despite the emotional toll on their team. Pahokee played furiously, holding the Rebels to a small halftime lead. In the third quarter though, Byrnes pulled ahead, winning 38–12.

Pahokee High finished its 2008 season with a 14–1 record as Florida's 2-B state champion for the third year in a row.

Central Gwinnett High School Black Knights
Suwannee, Georgia
Colors: Black and Gold
Georgia State Championships: Zero
Location, Date and Result: North Gwinnett High School;
September 14, 2009; Byrnes Won 43–7

When Byrnes signed a two-year deal with the Progressive Auto Football Challenge, the Rebs had to play rising national power North Gwinnett in 2008 and Central Gwinnett in 2009. Typically, out-of-state teams bring a string of recent success to the table, and the hope is that they will usually be a test. Central was none of the above.

Although managing to put points up first, Central could not handle the HPO (High Powered Offense) and Strike Force. Byrnes won the nationally televised game 43–7. The game was the first of a double-header. In the next game, North Gwinnett defeated Prattville (Alabama).

Byrnes ended its 2009 season with a 13–2 record as the state runner-up. Central Gwinnett went 2–8 that year.

St. Thomas Aquinas High School Raiders
Fort Lauderdale, Florida
Colors: Blue and Gold
Florida State Championships: Seven
Location, Date and Result: Lockhart Stadium, Fort Lauderdale;
December 2, 2009; STA won 42–35

None of Byrnes's out-of-state opponents had ever been able to match the Rebels' speed and strength, and the same can be said about any of Aquinas's opponents. When these two teams met, it was no. 1 STA versus no. 2 Byrnes, and the entire nation was watching. Ever since STA claimed Byrnes's no. 1 spot in the national polls in 2008, fans nationwide had wanted to see this game.

The two teams went back forth in the early part of the game, with STA taking the lead for most of the game. At times, it seemed as if the Rebels were ready to take the lead, only to have it slip away.

Unable to come back and win the game, Byrnes fought tooth and nail until the final buzzer. Filled with many breathtaking moments, most everyone agreed that this game could have went either way.

STA finished 13–1, losing in the state semifinals.

CHAPTER 6
CHAMPIONSHIP CATERIAL

SILVER BULLET: THE BYRNES HELMET PROJECT

(1) Byrnes's first helmet was dark blue with a thick gray stripe down the middle. Face masks were not used until 1956.

(2) The "Silver Bullet" was introduced in 1962 by Joe Hazle.

(3) In an effort to make their helmets stand out a little more, players applied a white stripe down the middle of the helmet, outlined by a blue strip on each side. Their numbers were also applied to each side of their helmet.

(4) For one season, Byrnes helmets incorporated a blue oval with a gray "B" in the center. Some players' helmets had one red star on each side of the center blue stripe. This style was only worn for one season.

(5) The year 1974 was the first time the color red was used prominently anywhere on the uniforms. This style was only worn for one season.

(6) Byrnes went back to the blue helmet with a white face mask in 1975.

(7) In 1978, Coach Corne kept the blue helmet but used a white script "B" on the helmet. This style was only worn for one season.

(8) The "Silver Bullet" made its return in 1980. The silver color and blue face mask has remained the core design ever since.

(9) The infamous Rebels logo is first used on the helmets. Although smaller, the logo looks very similar to the one used presently.

The Helmet Project. *Courtesy of the author.*

It had three stars representing the 1976, 1982 and 1986 state championship titles.

(10) Since 2000, the helmet has featured the Rebels logo exclusively without the blue helmet stripe from 1997–9. The logo has been updated with six red stars since the 2002 season.

BLUE AND GRAY (WITH A LITTLE RED FOR COLOR)

The Rebels have worn many variations of the jersey of the years. The jerseys have evolved numerous times, and each design seemed to reflect the trends of the time. Fans and players alike have their favorite Rebels jersey, and their reasons for doing so can vary.

So, do the jerseys from your time look the way you remember?

1955–8: Dark blue jersey, gray numbers.
1955–8: White jersey, blue numbers.
1958: White numbers on blue/white shoulders with stars on each side.
1959–61: Blue jersey, white numbers (Ole Miss style).

1959–62: White jersey, blue numbers (Ole Miss style).

1962–4: White jersey, blue numbers (Ole Miss style).

1963–4: White jersey, blue numbers.

1965–7: Blue jersey, white numbers (three white stripes on sleeves).

1965–7: White jersey, blue numbers (three blue stripes on sleeves).

1968–71 Blue jersey, white numbers (Ole Miss–style white shoulder stripes with pinstripe in the center).

1968–70: White jersey, blue numbers (Ole Miss–style blue shoulder stripes with pinstripe in the center).

1972–6: Blue jersey, white numbers (white and blue trim at ends of sleeves).

1971–3: White jersey, blue numbers. (Blue University of Southern California–style angled striped on shoulders; first Byrnes jersey with name bar on the back.)

1974: White jersey, blue numbers. (Three blue stripes on the sleeves; first jersey to have school name on it.)

1975: White jersey, blue numbers. While not the first jersey to have "Byrnes" on it, it is significant for being the first one to have "Byrnes" printed on the front; blue trim at end of sleeves.

1976–7: White jersey, blue shoulders, blue numbers. This jersey was worn during the 1976 state championship game.

1977–8: Blue jersey, white numbers (three white stripes on sleeves).

1977–8: White jersey, blue numbers (three blue stripes on sleeves).

1979: Blue jersey, white numbers.

1979: White jersey, blue numbers.

1980–3: Blue jersey, gray numbers with white trim (four stripes on sleeves, two gray, two white). Byrnes's staple jersey for year; red stars were added in 1984 through 1987; this jersey was brought back for the 1990 through 1993 seasons.

1980–3: White jersey, blue numbers with gray trim (four stripes on sleeves, two blue, two gray).

1984–7: The "Championship Jerseys." These jerseys were just like the jerseys used from 1980 to 1983 except for one small detail: There was a red star for each football championship won by Byrnes. There was one star on each side of the name. After the 1986 championship, a red star was added to the pants. The red star is still a tradition used today.

1988–9: Blue jersey, white numbers (three white stripes on sleeve). Away jersey featured the same design, but with the colors reversed.

1994–8: Blue jersey, white numbers with red outline (two white stripes on each side with red trim). It's the first jersey to feature red prominently.

1994–8: White jersey, blue numbers with red outline (two blue stripes on each side with red trim).

1999–2005: Blue jersey with white numbers and red trim, and "Byrnes" printed in a nontraditional style of lettering. The numbers were dimensional. Red numbers with white trim on shoulders.

1999–2000: White jersey with blue numbers, and "Byrnes" printed in a nontraditional style of lettering. Three-dimensional numbers in blue with red trim. The logo was used on the sleeves, outlined by pyramid-style lines.

2001–3: Throwback-style jersey. Featured blue shoulders, "Byrnes" printed in blue with red trim and three-dimensional numbers in blue with a white-and-bold-red outline. Numbers on shoulders printed in white with red trim. Rebels with three red stars printed in white on each sleeve.

2004–5: Featured blue shoulders with Byrnes, and the numbers printed in blue with red and trim. T.V. numbers on the sleeves in blue with red and white trim.

2005: Possibly Byrnes's most unique and least-used jersey. Gray with blue shoulders and blue side inserts. Red stripes across the top of the shoulders and red stripes on the front. Blue numbers with red trim. School name stitched in small letters in the front.

2006–present: With the school's Nike contract, the Rebels were outfitted in the best Nike had to offer. The current home jerseys are blue, with Byrnes and the numbers in white with red trim and red piping. The shoulders feature a gray stripe on each side with red and white trim.

2006–present: One of the Rebels' official Nike jerseys. This away uniform is white with blue numbers in red trim. The most intricate jersey to date, piping starts just above the school name and continues to each side of the shoulders, where the trim opens up to thick blue trim. A thick blue stripe runs up the sides of the jersey, flanked by two red stripes.

2008–present: This is the second gray jersey at Byrnes but the first jersey to feature gray so prominently. School name and numbers in blue with red trim, and blue stripes on the shoulders with red and white trim. Used as an away jersey, it has only been worn at the 2008 North Gwinnett, Gaffney and Dorman games.

CHAPTER 7

CHAMPIONSHIP RINGS

GOT RINGS?

Some athletes and coaches spend a lifetime trying to win a championship ring. At Byrnes, some coaches are running out of fingers to put them on. Like the school, the rings have changed and grown in size over the years.

The 2005, 2007 and 2008 state championship rings. *Courtesy of the author and Tony Gillespie.*

THE LOGO

When venturing through the District 5 community, it's not difficult to see the famous "Rebels" logo at any given moment. You can spot the logo on shirts, car decals, garden flags and even light posts down Main Street Duncan. Other schools have adopted our logo for themselves; however, the logo was ours from its inception and is now a point of pride at Byrnes.

In August 1991, the Huguenot Ad Agency of Spartanburg was hired to create a selection of images that would become the school mascot. With the 1991–2 school year drawing near, the Huguenot Agency submitted its designs, and the students were given a chance to vote on them.

On September 4, 1991, a ballot was submitted with four potential mascots. The designs included a dagger with the word "Rebels" embedded in the blade; a "Knight-like" figure riding a stallion; "Rebels" in script with a saber penetrating the bottom of the logo; and finally, the same script as above with a stallion's head over the logo.

In the initial vote, the current logo won 33 percent of the vote, with the knight coming in a close second-place finish. In a runoff vote, the logo we are all familiar with today once again won overall with 523 votes to the knight's 396.

The logo has been around nearly twenty years, and it has become a beloved and unique symbol of our school. The logo is used by all sports at Byrnes; however, the football team's helmet logo features a red star for every state championship that they have won. In 2002, the logo was slightly updated with a sleeker, more colorful design featuring red, white and blue as the colors.

CHAPTER 8
THE FUTURE

D.R. HILL AND FLORENCE CHAPEL

To get a glimpse of future Rebels, drop by a Florence Chapel or D.R. Hill game during the fall. The development of star-caliber athletes start at a young age in District 5. The skills that the players learn in D5 Rebel Youth League continue during middle school, and the coaches at the middle schools are cultivating future Rebels.

During summer workouts, the Tigers and Cougars learn about competition through seven-on-seven practices, weightlifting and, most recently, competing in seven-on-seven tournaments. All Tigers and Cougars strive to become Rebels one day, and with the encouragement of their families and coaches, most meet that goal.

The Tigers and Cougars compete in seven-on-seven scrimmages during the summer. Although the students at the two schools grow up together—attending church, camps and playing together in D5 football—for two games during the season, the meet in a heated rivalry game. It's in these matchups that coaches and players compete for bragging rights that carry into the summer workouts.

D.R. HILL TIGERS

Colors: Black, Gold and Silver
Founded: 1963

When people ask "Who was D.R. Hill?" most people cannot answer the question. D.R. Hill was a 1924 graduate of Furman University. Hired right out of college, Hill was the first and only superintendent of Duncan High School. He served Duncan High from 1924 until 1950.

For many years, D.R. Hill was the only middle school in District 5. Not many Byrnes alumni can share memories of their days as Rebels without remembering their days as "Tigers."

Don't be confused if you catch a DRH game and think you are watching another team. D.R. Hill still carries gold as an official color, but the football team has replaced the gold with silver and now proudly wears silver helmets.

FLORENCE CHAPEL COUGARS

Colors: Crimson and Silver
Founded: 2004

Opened in 2004, Florence Chapel was named after the former African American school in Wellford.

Florence Chapel serves students on the Reidville side of Interstate 85. Despite being in the same district and having identical buildings, Florence Chapel and DRH have their own unique identities.

Although the mascot of the original Florence Chapel was the Hornet, students were given a chance to vote and determine the new mascot and colors. The colors of crimson and silver along with the Cougar nickname won the vote.

At the end of the eighth-grade DRH–FC game, the players gather at midfield. At that time, the players are greeted by their current coaches and, usually, the Byrnes coaches. It is from that point that they are reminded that they are no longer "two teams," but that they are now Rebels.

CHAPTER 9
ALL-TEAM-PICTURES

1955. *Courtesy of Byrnes High School.*

Above: 1955.
*Courtesy of
Gerald Turner.*

Right: 1956.
*Courtesy of
Byrnes High
School.*

1957. *Courtesy of Byrnes High School.*

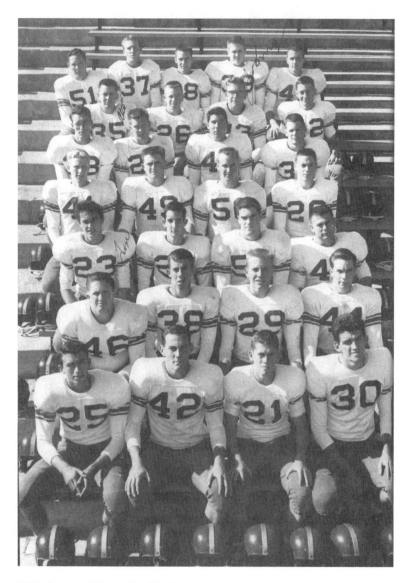

1958. *Courtesy of Byrnes High School.*

Above: 1959.
*Courtesy of
Byrnes High
School.*

Left: 1960.
*Courtesy of
Byrnes High
School.*

1961. *Courtesy of Byrnes High School.*

1962. *Courtesy of Byrnes High School.*

1963. *Courtesy of Byrnes High School.*

1964. *Courtesy of Byrnes High School.*

1965. *Courtesy of Byrnes High School.*

1966. *Courtesy of Byrnes High School.*

1967. *Courtesy of Byrnes High School.*

1968. *Courtesy of Byrnes High School.*

All-Team Pictures

1969. *Courtesy of Byrnes High School.*

1970. *Courtesy of Byrnes High School.*

1971. *Courtesy of Byrnes High School.*

1972. *Courtesy of Byrnes High School.*

1973. *Courtesy of Byrnes High School.*

1974. *Courtesy of Byrnes High School.*

1975. *Courtesy of Byrnes High School.*

1976. *Courtesy of Byrnes High School.*

1977. *Courtesy of Byrnes High School.*

1978. *Courtesy of Byrnes High School.*

1979. *Courtesy of Byrnes High School.*

1980. *Courtesy of Byrnes High School.*

All-Team Pictures

1981. *Courtesy of Byrnes High School.*

1982. *Courtesy of Byrnes High School.*

1983. *Courtesy of Byrnes High School.*

1984. *Courtesy of Byrnes High School.*

1985. *Courtesy of Byrnes High School.*

1986. *Courtesy of Byrnes High School.*

1987. *Courtesy of Byrnes High School.*

1988. *Courtesy of Byrnes High School.*

1989. *Courtesy of Byrnes High School.*

1990. *Courtesy of Byrnes High School.*

1991. *Courtesy of Byrnes High School.*

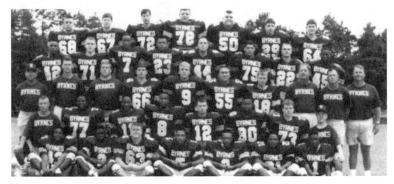

1992. *Courtesy of Byrnes High School.*

1993. *Courtesy of Byrnes High School.*

1994. *Courtesy of Byrnes High School.*

1995. *Courtesy of Byrnes High School.*

1996. *Courtesy of Byrnes High School.*

1997. *Courtesy of Byrnes High School.*

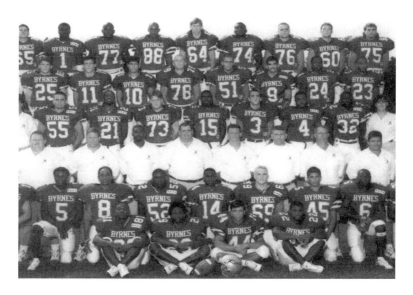

1998. *Courtesy of Byrnes High School.*

1999. *Courtesy of Byrnes High School.*

2000. *Courtesy of Byrnes High School.*

2001. *Courtesy of Byrnes High School.*

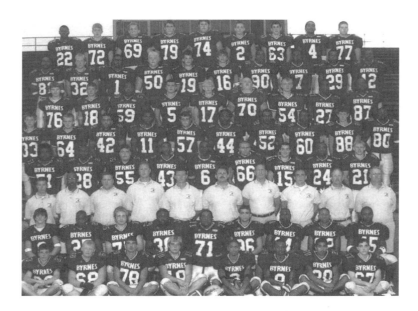

2002. *Courtesy of Byrnes High School.*

2003. *Courtesy of Byrnes High School.*

2004. *Courtesy of Byrnes High School.*

All-Team Pictures

2005. *Courtesy of Byrnes High School.*

2006. *Courtesy of Byrnes High School.*

2007. *Courtesy of Byrnes High School.*

2008. *Courtesy of Byrnes High School.*

2009. *Courtesy of Byrnes High School.*

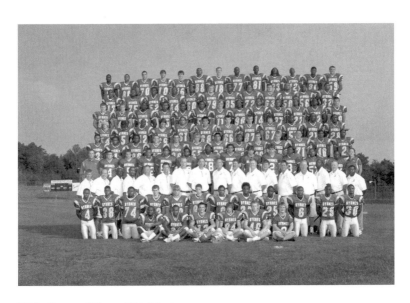

2010. *Courtesy of Byrnes High School.*

CHAPTER 10
ALL-TIME SEASON AND GAME-BY-GAME RESULTS

1955–PRESENT

Over the years, especially on Friday nights at Nixon Field, sometimes alumni and fans will debate the outcome of particular games or will debate which decade saw the best performance from the Rebels. On the next few pages, look back to when you played or when you went to Byrnes and compare *your Rebels* to other years.

In the next section, you will see what coaches led the Rebels in the respective decade and how many wins, losses and playoff appearances the Rebels have had.

1950s

Record: 30–17–5
Playoff Appearances: Two (1955, 1957)
Coaches: Charles Burnette (1955), H.L. Quintana (1956–8)
and Joe Hazle (1959–64)

1955 (6–3–2)

Byrnes			
	2	Clover	2
	43	Blue Ridge	13
	31	Boiling Springs	6
	19	Fairforest (Dorman)	13
	0	Woodruff	0
	20	Cowpens	12
	0	Laurens	6
	26	Chapman	7
	13	Travelers Rest	6
	12	Greer	60
	12	Olympia	32

1956 (7–3)

Byrnes			
	25	Clover	13
	20	Blue Ridge	0
	28	Boiling Springs	6
	6	Fairforest (Dorman)	19
	6	Woodruff	7
	19	Cowpens (Broome)	7
	26	Laurens	0
	40	Chapman	19
	20	Travelers Rest	0
	7	Greer	27

1957 (5–4–1)

Byrnes	7	Lexington	12
	19	Boiling Springs	0
	14	Fairforest (Dorman)	14
	6	Woodruff	13
	19	Cowpens (Broome)	7
	13	Laurens	6
	18	Chapman	6
	6	Carolina	0
	6	Greer	44
	0	Palmetto	6

1958 (5–4–1)

Byrnes	7	Lexington	25
	0	Woodruff	6
	0	Fairforest (Dorman)	14
	6	Union	6
	6	Easley	0
	13	Laurens	0
	6	Chapman	0
	14	Carolina	7
	6	Greer	13
	21	Palmetto	0

1959 (7–3–1)

Byrnes	0	Spartanburg	0
	6	Woodruff	0
	0	Fairforest (Dorman)	6
	7	Union	13
	22	Easley	7
	7	Laurens	6
	13	Chapman	6
	7	Carolina	0
	7	Greer	6
	31	Palmetto	0
	13	Lancaster	21

1960s

Record: 52–48–8
Playoff Appearances: Zero
Coaches: Joe Hazle (1959–64), Kermit Littlefield (1965–6) and
Dalton Rivers (1967–76)

1960 (7–1–2)

Byrnes			
	6	Spartanburg	7
	14	Woodruff	0
	26	Fairforest (Dorman)	0
	4	Union	0
	6	Easley	6
	34	Laurens	0
	7	Chapman	0
	21	Carolina	0
	0	Greer	0
	27	Palmetto	0

1961 (6–4–1)

Byrnes			
	19	Blue Ridge	0
	19	Spartanburg	0
	6	Woodruff	7
	6	Fairforest (Dorman)	6
	8	Union	7
	7	Easley	27
	14	Palmetto	0
	0	Daniel	31
	27	Chapman	7
	33	Carolina	0
	6	Greer	17

1962 (2–7–1)

Byrnes			
	0	Spartanburg	33
	0	Woodruff	18
	0	Dorman	7
	20	Blue Ridge	0
	0	Easley	25
	6	Daniel	39

0	Chapman	6
7	Carolina	7
6	Greer	20
6	Palmetto	0

1963 (9–2)

Byrnes	34	Pickens	0
	19	Spartanburg	13
	0	Woodruff	32
	20	Dorman	0
	28	Blue Ridge	0
	12	Easley	7
	19	Parker	7
	31	Chapman	7
	6	Carolina	0
	0	Greer	14
	25	Palmetto	12

1964 (8–3)

Byrnes	20	Pickens	7
	7	Spartanburg	14
	9	Woodruff	7
	19	Dorman	0
	29	Blue Ridge	0
	7	Easley	20
	14	Parker	12
	25	Chapman	0
	20	Hillcrest	0
	14	Greer	27
	7	Palmetto	0

1965 (3–7–1)

Byrnes	25	Pickens	0
	7	Spartanburg	6
	0	Woodruff	45
	7	Dorman	7
	2	Berkeley	13
	0	Easley	7
	7	Parker	14

	34	Chapman	0
	12	Hillcrest	32
	0	Greer	3
	0	Palmetto	18

1966 (2–8–1)

Byrnes	0	Pickens	18
	6	Spartanburg	7
	6	Woodruff	6
	0	Dorman	12
	0	Belton-Honea Path	42
	7	Easley	21
	0	Parker	14
	7	Chapman	0
	21	Hillcrest	13
	6	Greer	7
	12	Palmetto	20

1967 (3–7–1)

Byrnes	21	Pickens	20
	19	Spartanburg	19
	2	Woodruff	49
	0	Dorman	21
	0	Belton-Honea Path	40
	0	Easley	40
	20	Parker	34
	27	Chapman	7
	14	Hillcrest	6
	0	Greer	12
	12	Palmetto	31

1968 (7–4)

Byrnes	20	Seneca	0
	13	Spartanburg	35
	0	Woodruff	14
	21	Dorman	7
	0	Belton-Honea Path	20
	6	Easley	14
	7	J.L. Mann	0

	Chapman	
52	Chapman	0
27	Daniel	7
21	Greer	13
20	Palmetto	6

1969 (5–5–1)

Byrnes			
	39	Seneca	8
	6	Spartanburg	15
	6	Woodruff	6
	14	Dorman	21
	10	Belton-Honea Path	7
	18	Easley	26
	26	J.L. Mann	0
	46	Chapman	0
	3	Daniel	7
	3	Greer	27
	43	Hillcrest	6

1970s

Record: 66–39–4
Playoff Appearances: Two (1975, 1976)
State Championships: One (1976)
Region Titles: One (1975)
Coaches: Dalton Rivers (1967–76) and Bo Corne (1977–86)

1970 (7–3–1)

Byrnes			
	27	Chapman	0
	6	Spartanburg	20
	14	Woodruff	22
	7	Gaffney	6
	35	Dorman	0
	49	Southside	0
	7	Union	0
	40	Chester	6
	0	Rock Hill	0
	6	Lancaster	19
	32	Greer	0

1971 (4–6–1)

Byrnes	25	Chapman	0
	7	Spartanburg	35
	0	Woodruff	13
	23	Gaffney	13
	9	Dorman	10
	14	Southside	6
	0	Union	19
	14	Chester	14
	7	Rock Hill	13
	14	Lancaster	35
	27	Greer	7

1972 (8–2)

Byrnes	17	Parker	0
	20	Spartanburg	14
	0	Dorman	7
	15	Woodruff	0
	8	Clinton	17
	19	York	0
	26	Chapman	0
	26	Boiling Springs	0
	22	Clover	18
	19	Greer	7

1973 (7–4)

Byrnes	32	Parker	7
	12	Spartanburg	26
	28	Dorman	6
	14	Woodruff	0
	50	Riverside	0
	0	Clinton	22
	20	York	13
	33	Chapman	7
	32	Boiling Springs	8
	20	Clover	24
	14	Greer	26

1974 (8–3)

Byrnes			
	28	Dorman	0
	0	Spartanburg	50
	8	Woodruff	0
	19	Clover	13
	6	York	7
	48	Riverside	0
	33	Boiling Springs	0
	39	Mauldin	6
	22	Chapman	0
	7	Clinton	12
	34	Greer	18

1975 (6–5)

Byrnes			
	18	Dorman	20
	7	Spartanburg	14
	13	Woodruff	17
	7	Clover	0
	6	York	7
	47	Riverside	0
	19	Boiling Springs	0
	21	Mauldin	0
	34	Chapman	0
	14	Clinton	6
	22	Pageland	23

1976 (12–1–1), state champions

Byrnes			
	21	Dorman	15
	6	Spartanburg	0
	0	Woodruff	0
	41	Broome	0
	21	Boiling Springs	0
	6	York	0
	27	Greer	13
	7	Clinton	9
	28	Riverside	3
	39	Southside	0
	32	Seneca	0
	43	Batesburg-Leesville	0

	34	Newberry	7
	34	Bishop England	0

1977 (3–6–1)

Byrnes	0	Dorman	7
	0	Spartanburg	20
	6	Woodruff	6
	13	Broome	21
	28	Boiling Springs	8
	0	York	10
	21	Greer	27
	0	Clinton	28
	36	Riverside	0
	35	Southside	0

1978 (6–4)

Byrnes	21	Dorman	41
	8	Greer	7
	14	Woodruff	21
	38	Eastside	13
	23	Laurens	20
	7	Westside	0
	6	T.L. Hanna	13
	28	Easley	0
	19	Wade Hampton	13
	0	Greenwood	36

1979 (5–5)

Byrnes	18	Dorman	3
	7	Greer	13
	0	Woodruff	9
	0	Eastside	7
	7	Laurens	8
	24	Westside	0
	7	T.L. Hanna	21
	35	Easley	6
	21	Wade Hampton	6
	21	Greenwood	16

1980s

Record: 80–39–1
Playoff Appearances: Seven (1982, 1983, 1984, 1985, 1986, 1987, 1989)
State Championships: Two (1982 and 1986)
Upper State Championships: One (1985)
Region Titles: One (1983)
Coaches: Bo Corne (1977–86), Keith McAlister (1987–8) and Fred Coan (1989–94)

1980 (6–4)

Byrnes	21	Boiling Springs	0
	8	Dorman	10
	13	Woodruff	16
	14	Greer	7
	42	Riverside	0
	21	J.L. Mann	3
	7	Clinton	23
	21	Southside	14
	6	Broome	9
	35	Mauldin	0

1981 (5–4–1)

Byrnes	0	Boiling Springs	0
	9	Dorman	15
	21	Woodruff	19
	0	Greer	7
	27	Riverside	10
	22	J.L. Mann	21
	14	Clinton	27
	15	Southside	12
	7	Broome	27
	28	Mauldin	26

1982 (12–2), state champions

Byrnes	14	Dorman	3
	28	Riverside	9
	40	Parker	0
	16	Southside	0
	0	Greer	7
	20	Carolina	0
	34	Berea	7
	29	Woodmont	7
	14	J.L. Mann	16
	14	Woodruff	9
	27	T.L. Hanna	6
	14	Broome	9
	10	Seneca	0
	9	Myrtle Beach	6

1983 (9–3)

Byrnes	14	Dorman	0
	12	Riverside	9
	7	Parker	15
	27	Southside	3
	27	Greer	14
	28	Carolina	0
	27	Berea	7
	42	Woodmont	0
	30	J.L. Mann	0
	14	Woodruff	21
	6	Newberry	0
	0	Seneca	10

1984 (9–3)

Byrnes	41	Greer	7
	28	Westside	2
	27	Wade Hampton	14
	39	Northwestern	20
	14	Spartanburg	33
	3	Gaffney	14
	28	Rock Hill	0
	21	Union	7

14	Boiling Springs	7
21	Dorman	14
47	Mauldin	0
20	Laurens	28

1985 (10–4)

Byrnes	41	Greer	7
	41	Westside	10
	34	Wade Hampton	0
	16	Northwestern	0
	6	Spartanburg	9
	6	Gaffney	7
	10	Rock Hill	18
	29	Union	3
	31	Boiling Springs	6
	21	Dorman	5
	10	Union	6
	25	Brookland Cayce	0
	14	Airport	0
	13	Hillcrest-Dalzell	14

1986 (11–3), state champions

Byrnes	10	Greer	0
	34	Westside	6
	32	J.L. Mann	6
	31	Northwestern	13
	3	Spartanburg	12
	13	Gaffney	16
	28	Rock Hill	0
	6	Union	7
	34	Boiling Springs	7
	37	Dorman	0
	28	Westside	6
	11	Boiling Springs	0
	24	Airport	17
	41	Berkeley	14

1987 (6–5)

Byrnes	22	Greer	21
	20	Westside	3
	13	J.L. Mann	7
	0	Northwestern	25
	13	Spartanburg	29
	17	Gaffney	20
	16	Rock Hill	0
	6	Union	0
	41	Boiling Springs	8
	0	Dorman	22
	7	Brookland Cayce	14

1988 (6–5)

Byrnes	14	Dorman	9
	7	Spartanburg	28
	26	Westside	7
	21	Union	14
	20	Greenville	3
	20	Woodmont	23
	0	Broome	13
	13	Riverside	14
	21	Greer	10
	0	Berea	15
	25	J.L. Mann	24

1989 (6–6)

Byrnes	7	Dorman	28
	7	Spartanburg	22
	10	Westside	0
	0	Union	20
	34	Greenville	6
	17	Woodmont	0
	35	Broome	6
	14	Riverside	21
	0	Greer	14
	21	Berea	0
	41	J.L. Mann	0
	0	Camden	33

1990s

Record: 49–68
Playoff Appearances: Five (1993, 1994, 1996, 1997, 1998)
Region Titles: One (1993)
Coaches: Fred Coan (1989–94) and Bobby Bentley (1995–2006)

1990 (2–9)

Byrnes			
	0	Dorman	24
	21	Spartanburg	7
	13	Woodruff	20
	0	Union	36
	34	Greenville	0
	0	Woodmont	14
	12	Broome	28
	16	Riverside	33
	7	Greer	34
	3	Berea	7
	23	J.L. Mann	24

1991 (7–4)

Byrnes			
	13	Dorman	7
	3	Spartanburg	21
	21	Woodruff	14
	7	Union	10
	37	Greenville	0
	23	Woodmont	0
	10	Broome	0
	49	Riverside	6
	3	Greer	28
	14	Berea	38
	22	J.L. Mann	3

1992 (3–8)

Byrnes			
	10	Greer	0
	3	Spartanburg	34
	3	Dorman	12

14	Union	47
0	Westside	34
3	Greenwood	35
0	Laurens	56
35	Hillcrest	13
13	Pickens	21
7	Easley	34
46	Mauldin	14

1993 (10–2)

Byrnes	24	Greer	21
	0	Spartanburg	10
	28	Dorman	21
	18	Union	17
	35	Westside	28
	28	Greenwood	13
	27	Laurens	7
	52	Hillcrest	8
	35	Pickens	18
	28	Easley	6
	35	Mauldin	23
	17	Dillon	21

1994 (6–6)

Byrnes	10	Greer	20
	10	Spartanburg	28
	21	Dorman	45
	9	Union	21
	31	Westside	28
	28	Greenwood	21
	14	Laurens	26
	20	Hillcrest	14
	14	Pickens	7
	21	Easley	0
	35	Mauldin	8
	6	Dillon	20

1995 (2–9)

Byrnes	7	Greer	38
	0	Spartanburg	42
	6	Dorman	42
	0	Union	54
	7	Westside	35
	6	Greenwood	35
	6	Laurens	41
	14	Hillcrest	21
	22	Pickens	7
	12	Easley	22
	34	Mauldin	20

1996 (1–11)

Byrnes	10	Eastside	27
	6	Greer	28
	21	Mauldin	26
	30	T.L. Hanna	20
	7	Gaffney	28
	13	Dorman	17
	0	Aiken	17
	13	Rock Hill	38
	14	Spartanburg	35
	6	Northwestern	70
	12	Boiling Springs	28
	7	Berkeley	21

1997 (8–5)

Byrnes	31	Eastside	7
	42	Greer	27
	46	Mauldin	27
	49	T.L. Hanna	14
	17	Gaffney	42
	7	Dorman	35
	28	Aiken	14
	7	Rock Hill	31
	31	Spartanburg	25
	10	Northwestern	26
	28	Boiling Springs	6

	24	Lancaster	19
	25	Hartsville	34

1998 (7–6)

Byrnes	68	Eastside	22
	52	Greer	3
	70	Mauldin	6
	65	T.L. Hanna	6
	21	Gaffney	34
	20	Dorman	31
	35	Laurens	14
	28	Rock Hill	29
	21	Spartanburg	35
	17	Northwestern	31
	35	Boiling Springs	21
	49	Berkeley	14
	6	Ridge View	7

1999 (3–8)

Byrnes	28	Eastside	27
	14	Greer	34
	38	Mauldin	27
	54	T.L. Hanna	14
	9	Gaffney	42
	28	Dorman	45
	7	Laurens	25
	0	Rock Hill	41
	6	Spartanburg	38
	7	Northwestern	45
	17	Boiling Springs	21

2000s

Record: 128–16
Playoff Appearances: Ten (2000, 2001, 2002, 2003, 2004,
2005, 2006, 2007, 2008, 2009)
State Championships: Six (2002, 2003, 2004, 2005, 2007, 2008)
Upper State Championships: One (2009)
Region Titles: Six (2002, 2003, 2004, 2005, 2007, 2009)
Coaches: Bobby Bentley (1995–2006) and Chris Miller
(2007–Present)

2000 (8–5)

Byrnes	35	Eastside	7
	27	Greer	28
	31	Orangeburg-Wilk.	22
	48	T.L. Hanna	0
	24	Gaffney	23
	3	Dorman	41
	16	Rock Hill	28
	10	Northwestern	28
	35	Fort Mill	6
	24	Spartanburg	21
	37	Boiling Springs	7
	23	Conway	20
	17	Marlboro County	21

2001 (10–4)

Byrnes	51	Eastside	0
	24	Greer	7
	36	Orangeburg-Wilk.	7
	65	T.L. Hanna	14
	17	Gaffney	7
	16	Dorman	17
	7	Rock Hill	0
	13	Northwestern	21
	52	Fort Mill	13
	26	Spartanburg	27

41	Boiling Springs	3
49	James Island	14
45	Crestwood	19
14	Conway	19

2002 (14–1), state champions

Byrnes	41	Aiken	22
	28	Greer	15
	34	Mauldin	7
	10	Evangel Christian (LA)	21
	62	Easley	7
	35	Greenwood	22
	42	Gaffney	7
	31	Dorman	13
	40	Laurens	7
	26	Spartanburg	15
	52	Boiling Springs	6
	42	Crestwood	7
	54	Battery Creek	6
	15	Mauldin	7
	34	Conway	28

2003 (15–0), state champions

Byrnes	45	Aiken	21
	42	Greer	29
	45	Mauldin	28
	27	Northwestern	24
	35	Easley	14
	48	Greenwood	28
	42	Gaffney	14
	28	Dorman	7
	47	Laurens	7
	34	Spartanburg	24
	45	Boiling Springs	8
	52	South Florence	35
	31	Greenwood	14
	51	Berkeley	22
	40	Conway	14

2004 (13–1), state champions

Byrnes	74	Eastside	7
	50	Greer	20
	28	J.L. Mann	14
	10	Gaffney	12
	35	Greenwood	14
	47	Spartanburg	7
	49	Hillcrest	0
	21	Dorman	19
	65	Mauldin	7
	63	Boiling Springs	14
	45	South Aiken	3
	28	T.L. Hanna	7
	56	Aiken	29
	35	Irmo	7

2005 (15–0), state champions

Byrnes	62	MBA (TN)	14
	68	Eastside	7
	56	Greer	0
	65	J.L. Mann	6
	30	Gaffney	10
	62	Greenwood	34
	55	Spartanburg	10
	44	Hillcrest	0
	45	Dorman	17
	51	Mauldin	0
	56	Boiling Springs	7
	45	Laurens	20
	45	York	0
	42	Aiken	14
	51	Richland Northeast	8

2006 (11–2)

Byrnes	55	Hartsville	20
	27	Glades Central (FL)	15
	41	Greer	6
	21	Moeller (OH)	20
	45	Dorman	7

55	Spartanburg	17
71	Hillcrest	9
42	Clover	13
15	Gaffney	28
52	Mauldin	6
52	Boiling Springs	0
56	Wando	7
13	Gaffney	16

2007 (15–0), state champions

Byrnes	55	Hartsville	28
	45	Greer	7
	18	Dr. Phillips (FL)	14
	38	Centerville (OH)	31
	31	Dorman	17
	63	Spartanburg	9
	38	Hillcrest	20
	28	Clover	12
	49	Gaffney	14
	41	Mauldin	31
	62	Boiling Springs	0
	56	Hillcrest	14
	31	Dorman	14
	14	Northwestern	0
	48	Summerville	9

2008 (14–1), state champions

Byrnes	37	N. Gwinnett (GA)	21
	45	Ridge View	20
	63	Greer	0
	38	Lincoln (FL)	31
	42	Gaffney	14
	38	Pahokee (FL)	12
	39	Spartanburg	3
	48	Hillcrest	7
	28	Dorman	38
	70	Mauldin	27
	42	Boiling Springs	6
	34	Spartanburg	0

	48	Clover	7
	24	Dorman	13
	31	Sumter	21

2009 (13–2)

Byrnes	43	C. Gwinnett (GA)	7
	65	Myrtle Beach	14
	52	Greer	6
	85	Woodland	8
	60	Gaffney	7
	34	Aquinas (FL)	42
	49	Spartanburg	6
	42	Hillcrest	9
	17	Dorman	10
	72	Mauldin	27
	53	Boiling Springs	0
	58	White Knoll	0
	68	Mauldin	28
	58	Spartanburg	16
	17	Dorman	28

2010 regular season (8–3)

Byrnes	0	Hoover (AL)	14
	21	Myrtle Beach	14
	52	Forestview (NC)	6
	16	Gaffney	26
	40	TL Hanna	18
	27	Mauldin	24
	37	Riverside	9
	54	JL Mann	0
	77	Hillcrest	7
	14	Dorman	21
	38	Boiling Springs	21

YEARLY RESULTS

661 Games Played

Year	Won	Loss	Tie	Percentage
1955	6	3	2	0.667
1956	7	3	0	0.700
1957	5	4	1	0.556
1958	5	4	1	0.556
1959	7	3	1	0.700
1960	7	1	2	0.875
1961	6	4	1	0.600
1962	2	7	1	0.222
1963	9	2	0	0.818
1964	8	3	0	0.727
1965	3	7	1	0.300
1966	2	8	1	0.200
1967	3	7	1	0.300
1968	7	4	0	0.636
1969	5	5	1	0.500
1970	7	3	1	0.700
1971	4	6	1	0.400
1972	8	2	0	0.800
1973	7	4	0	0.636
1974	8	3	0	0.727
1975	6	5	0	0.545
1976	12	1	1	0.923
1977	3	6	1	0.333
1978	6	4	0	0.600
1979	5	5	0	0.500
1980	6	4	0	0.600
1981	5	4	1	0.556
1982	12	2	0	0.857
1983	9	3	0	0.750
1984	9	3	0	0.750
1985	10	4	0	0.714
1986	11	3	0	0.786
1987	6	5	0	0.545
1988	6	5	0	0.545

All-Time Season and Game-by-Game Results

1989	6	6	0	0.500
1990	2	9	0	0.182
1991	7	4	0	0.636
1992	3	8	0	0.273
1993	10	2	0	0.833
1994	6	6	0	0.500
1995	2	9	0	0.182
1996	1	11	0	0.083
1997	8	5	0	0.615
1998	7	6	0	0.538
1999	3	8	0	0.273
2000	8	5	0	0.615
2001	10	4	0	0.714
2002	14	1	0	0.933
2003	15	0	0	1.000
2004	13	1	0	0.929
2005	15	0	0	1.000
2006	11	2	0	0.846
2007	15	0	0	1.000
2008	14	1	0	0.933
2009	13	2	0	0.923
2010 (regular season)	8	3	0	0.727
Total	**413**	**230**	**18**	**0.667**

Rebels versus All Opponents

661 Games Played

Team	Won	Loss	Tie	Percentage
Aiken	5	1	0	0.833
Airport	2	0	0	1.000
Aquinas (FL)	0	1	0	0.000
Batesburg-Leesville	1	0	0	1.000
Battery Creek	1	0	0	1.000
Belton-Honea Path	1	3	0	0.250
Berea	3	3	0	0.500
Berkeley	3	2	0	0.600
Bishop England	1	0	0	1.000

Blue Ridge	6	0	0	1.000
Boiling Springs	28	2	1	0.928
Brookland Cayce	1	1	0	0.500
Broome	7	5	0	0.583
Camden	0	1	0	0.000
Carolina	8	0	1	1.000
Central Gwinnett (GA)	1	0	0	1.000
Centerville (OH)	1	0	0	1.000
Chapman	20	1	0	0.952
Chester	1	0	1	1.000
Clinton	1	7	0	0.125
Clover	7	1	1	0.875
Conway	3	1	0	0.750
Crestwood	2	0	0	1.000
Daniel	0	3	0	0.000
Dillon	0	1	0	0.000
Dorman (Fairforest)	28	27	3	0.508
Dr. Phillips (FL)	1	0	0	1.000
Easley	9	10	1	0.474
Eastside	8	2	0	0.800
Evangel Christian	0	1	0	0.000
Forestview (NC)	1	0	0	1.000
Fort Mill	2	0	0	1.000
Gaffney	10	12	0	0.450
Glades Central (FL)	1	0	0	1.000
Greenville	4	0	0	1.000
Greenwood	8	3	0	0.727
Greer	27	26	1	0.500
Hartsville	2	1	0	0.667
Hillcrest	16	2	0	0.870
Hillcrest-Dalzell	0	2	0	0.000
Hoover (AL)	0	1	0	0.000
Irmo	1	0	0	1.000
J.L. Mann	13	2	0	0.857
James Island	1	0	0	1.000
Lancaster	1	3	0	0.250
Laurens	11	7	0	0.611
Lexington	0	2	0	0.000
Lincoln (FL)	1	0	0	1.000

Marlboro County	0	1	0	0.000
Mauldin	23	1	0	0.952
Moeller (OH)	1	0	0	1.000
Montgomery Bell (TN)	1	0	0	1.000
Myrtle Beach	3	0	0	1.000
Newberry	2	0	0	1.000
North Gwinnett (GA)	1	0	0	1.000
Northwestern	5	7	0	0.417
Olympia	0	1	0	0.000
Orangeburg-Wilkinson	2	0	0	1.000
Pageland	0	1	0	0.000
Pahokee (FL)	1	0	0	1.000
Palmetto	8	4	0	0.667
Parker	5	4	0	0.556
Pickens	8	2	0	0.800
Richland Northeast	1	0	0	1.000
Ridge View	1	1	0	0.500
Riverside	11	3	0	0.769
Rock Hill	4	7	1	0.364
Seneca	3	1	0	0.750
South Aiken	1	0	0	1.000
South Florence	1	0	0	1.000
Southside	8	0	0	1.000
Spartanburg	18	27	2	0.370
Summerville	1	0	0	1.000
Sumter	1	0	0	1.000
T.L. Hanna	9	2	0	0.800
Traveler's Rest	2	0	0	1.000
Union	9	9	1	0.500
Wade Hampton	4	0	0	1.000
Wando	1	0	0	1.000
Westside	11	2	0	0.846
White Knoll	1	0	0	1.000
Woodland	1	0	0	1.000
Woodmont	4	2	0	0.667
Woodruff	9	17	5	0.346
York	4	3	0	0.571
Totals	**413**	**230**	**18**	**0.667**

BYRNES REBELS ALL-TIME CHAMPIONSHIP SUMMARY

All-time record: 413–230–18

Classifications: 2-AA, 3-AAA, 4-AAAA Division II, 4-AAAA Division I

Playoff appearances: Twenty-six (1955, 1957, 1975, 1976, 1982, 1983, 1984, 1985, 1986, 1987, 1989, 1993, 1994, 1996, 1997, 1998, 2000, 2001, 2002, 2003, 2004, 2005, 2006, 2007, 2008, 2009, 2010)

Region championships: Eight (1975 Peach Blossom 3-AAA; 1983 Peach Blossom 3-AAA; 1993 Region 1 4-AAAA; and 2002, 2004, 2005, 2007, 2009 Region II 4-AAAA)

Upper state championships: Two (1985 4-AAAA Division II and 2009 4-AAAA Division I)

State championships: Nine (1976 and 1982 3-AAA; 1986, 2002, 2003, 2004 and 2005 4-AAAA Division II; and 2007 and 2008 4-AAAA Division I)

Record at state championship: 9–2

CHAPTER 11
ALL=TIME RECORDS

TOP PERFORMANCES IN BYRNES FOOTBALL

Byrnes has had its share of record-breaking performances. Not only have the young men been able to break school records, some of these records have also, at some point, been South Carolina records. In the next few pages, you will find the names of players who have separated themselves from their peers and managed to etch their names in the record books.

Top Passing Yards in a Game

Date	Name	Opp.	COMP-ATT-INT	YD	TD
10/05/07	Chas Dodd	Hillcrest High School	18-40-0	462	4*
09/14/01	Anthony Johnson	TL Hanna High School	15-20-1	452	8
09/26/03	Trey Elder	Easley High School	29-42-1	447	5
11/24/03	Trey Elder	Berkeley High School	32-46-1	445	4

Date	Name	Opp.	COMP-ATT-INT	YD	TD
08/26/05	Willy Korn	Eastside High School	22-24-0	435	6
11/09/84	Steve Betsill	Mauldin High School	26-30-0	402	5
10/19/07	Chas Dodd	Gaffney High School	24-37-3	373	7
11/02/08	Chas Dodd	Mauldin High School	22-35-1	366	3
09/13/02	Justin Fulbright	Mauldin High School	13-19-0	363	4
10/27/06	Willy Korn	Mauldin High School	23-40-0	351	5

* Several more players hold this record.

Top Passing Yards in a Season

Year	Name	Games	COMP-ATT-INT	YD	TD
2009	Chas Dodd	15	252-391-7	4,169	51
2005	Willy Korn	15	281-421-6	4,164	53
2003	Trey Elder	15	242-349-9	3,728	35
2006	Willy Korn	13	253-380-10	3,485	39
2002	Justin Fulbright	15	191-318-8	3,320	34
2007	Chas Dodd	15	227-409-13	3,202	32
2004	Willy Korn	14	239-373-9	2,977	31
2008	Chas Dodd	15	213-383-11	2,927	28

All-Time Records

Year	Name	Games	COMP-ATT-INT	YD	TD
2001	Anthony Johnson	14	143-295-11	2,757	32
1984	Steve Betsill	12	213-343-9	2,748	25

Top Passing Yards in a Career

Years	Name	Games	COMP-ATT-INT	YD	TD
2006–9	Chas Dodd	53	763-1240-33	10,640	113
2003–6	Willy Korn	42	773-1174-25	10,626	123
1995–8	Tony Lane	44	326-669-30	5,230	69
1992–4	Brian Lane	31	355-626-23	5,068	53
1999–2001	Anthony Johnson	30	262-560-29	4,642	43
2000–2	Justin Fulbright	15	254-414-12	4,068	41
1982–4	Steve Betsill	25	322-565-24	4,424	38
2002–3	Trey Elder	15	247-354-9	3,830	36
1984–5	Bobby Bentley	15	166-340-18	2,360	20
1988–9	Jerry West	21	142-314-27	2,105	15

Longest Touchdown Passes

Year	From/To	Opp.	YD
1987	Archie Irby to Fred Davis	J.L. Mann High School	97
1998	Tony Lane to Durell Robinson	Eastside High School	94

Year	From/To	Opp.	YD
2001	Anthony Johnson to Travis Anderson	Fort Mill High School	89
2002	Justin Fulbright to Bradley Robinson	Greer High School	88
2005	Willy Korn to Jamar Anderson	Aiken High School	87
2007	Chas Dodd to Randall Hawkins	Hillcrest High School	82
1993	Brian Lane to O'Neil Gray	Laurens High School	81
2004	Willy Korn to Jamar Anderson	Eastside High School	80
2001	Anthony Johnson to Bradley Robinson	Spartanburg High School	80
1985	Bobby Bentley to Joey Bivens	Westside High School	80

Most Receptions in a Season

Year	Name	REC	YD	TD
2003	Jamar Wright	103	1,824	20
1984	Kelvin Richardson	97	1,334	14
2005	Jamar Anderson	96	1,748	20
2006	Randall Hawkins	85	1,262	17
2005	Matt Quinn	77	1,038	15
2002	Bradley Robinson	73	1,414	20
1998	Durell Robinson	73	1,386	23
2004	Reynaldo Hunter	71	1,098	13
2004	Freddie Brown	68	865	14
1985	Joey Bivens	67	1,048	9

Most Receptions in a Game

Year	Name	Opp.	REC	YD	TD
2003	Jamar Wright	Berkeley High School	14	233	2
1983	Kelvin Richardson	Woodruff High School	13	171	1
2003	Jamar Wright	Easley High School	12	188	4
1984	Kelvin Richardson	Laurens High School	11	220	1
1993	Abdul Davis	Hillcrest High School	11	202	2
2006	Xavier Dye	Gaffney High School	11	138	0
2003	Jamar Wright	Gaffney High School	11	130	1
2007	Ricco Sanders	Centerville High School	11	130	2
2005	Jamar Anderson	Greenwood High School	11	120	1
1984	Kelvin Richardson	Greer High School	11	119	2

Top Rushing Games: Yards

Year	Name	Opp.	ATT	YD	TD
2008	Marcus Lattimore	Sumter High School (state)	38	305	4
2007	Marcus Lattimore	Mauldin High School	25	269	4

Year	Name	Opp.	ATT	YD	TD
2008	Marcus Lattimore	Dorman High School (semifinals)	37	268	2
2007	Marcus Lattimore	Northwestern (semifinals)	41	240	2
2008	Marcus Lattimore	Ridgeview High School	18	233	3
2004	Rod Williams	Aiken High School	17	228	3
1973	Robert Meadows	Clover High School	N/A	227	N/A
1985	Tony Rogers	Boiling Springs High School	22	224	1
1998	Bennie Wright	Laurens High School	21	218	2
2008	Marcus Lattimore	Gaffney High School	21	209	2

Most Rushing Yards in a Season

Year	Name	Games	ATT	YD	TD
2008	Marcus Lattimore	15	305	2,303	30
2009	Marcus Lattimore	15	260	1,898	31
2007	Marcus Lattimore	15	284	1,836	26
1976	Mike Peake	14	N/A	1,536	N/A
1976	Mike Glenn	14	N/A	1,275	N/A
2004	Rodricuz Williams	14	175	1,177	13
2003	Rodricuz Williams	15	183	1,158	18
1993	Tyrone Foster	12	N/A	1,112	12
1983	Fred Irby	12	1,090	N/A	
1985	Tony Rogers	14	230	1,057	15

Longest Touchdown Runs

Year	Name	Opp.	YD
1974	Mike Glenn	Clover High School	97
1998	Bennie Wright	Eastside High School	91
1997	Tony Lane	Aiken High School	86
2005	Willy Korn	Greenwood High School	84
2008	Marcus Lattimore	Gaffney High School	71
2008	Marcus Lattimore	Sumter High School (state)	69
1994	Brian Lane	Mauldin High School	67
2006	Deonte Gist	Spartanburg High School	63
2005	Derek Young	Hillcrest High School	63
1995	Elton James	Pickens High School	60

Most Interceptions in a Game

Year	Name	Opp.	INT
1982	Tim Maybin	T.L. Hanna High School	3
1985	Bobby Peake	Hillcrest High School	3
2000	Travis Anderson	T.L. Hanna High School	3

Most Interceptions in a Season

Year	Name	INT	YD	TD
1983	Scott Simmons	13	101	1
1986	Matthew Smith	9	151	0
1986	Brad Stroble	9	99	0
2007	Riyahd Richardson	8	N/A	N/A

Year	Name	INT	YD	TD
2000	Travis Anderson	8	78	0
1976	Marshall Anderson	8	N/A	N/A
1973	Terry Moore	8	N/A	N/A
1986	Lamar Davis	7	99	2
1989	Reggie Scott	6	126	1
2005	Prince Miller	5	N/A	0

Longest Fumble Returns for Touchdowns

Year	Name	Opp.	YD
1988	Gregg Satterfield	Greer High School	93
2006	Everette Dawkins	Clover High School	89
1997	Maurice Sullivan	Hartsville High School	87
1983	Marvin Wright	Greer High School	65
2001	Josh Brock	Eastside High School	61
2005	Prince Miller	Aiken High School	44
1984	Tony Rogers	Dorman High School	43

INDIVIDUAL SCHOOL RECORDS

Rushing

RECORD

Amount	Name	Opponent	Year

YARDS IN A GAME
247   Rodricuz Williams   S. Florence High School   2003

YARDS IN A SEASON
1,536   Mike Peake   N/A   1976

YARDS IN A CAREER
6,375   Marcus Lattimore   N/A   2006–9

ATTEMPTS IN A GAME
34   Tyrone Foster   Dorman High School   1994

ATTEMPTS IN A SEASON
273   John Robinson   N/A   1982

ATTEMPTS IN A CAREER
Marcus Lattimore   N/A   2006–9

LONGEST RUN FROM SCRIMMAGE
97   Mike Glenn   Clover High School   1974

TOUCHDOWNS IN A GAME
4   Everette Dempsey   Laurens High School   1956
4   Marcus Lattimore   Mauldin High School   2008
3   Everett Dempsey   Chapman High School   1956
3   Ray Johnson   Hillcrest High School   1969
* several more players

TOUCHDOWNS IN A SEASON
31   Marcus Lattimore   N/A   2009

TOUCHDOWNS RUSHING IN A CAREER
320   Rodricuz Williams   N/A   2003–4

Passing

RECORD			
Amount	**Name**	**Opponent**	**Year**

MOST COMPLETIONS IN A GAME
32   Trey Elder   Berkeley High School   2003

RECORD

Amount	Name	Opponent	Year
COMPLETIONS IN A SEASON			
281	Willy Korn	N/A	2005
253	Willy Korn	N/A	2006
COMPLETIONS IN A CAREER			
773	Willy Korn	N/A	2003–6
ATTEMPTS IN A GAME			
53	Archie Irby	Union High School	1986
ATTEMPTS IN A SEASON			
358	Archie Irby	N/A	1986
ATTEMPTS IN A CAREER			
1,209	Chas Dodd (53 games)	N/A	2006–9
YARDS IN A GAME			
452	Anthony Johnson	T.L. Hanna High School	2000
YARDS IN A SEASON			
4,169	Chas Dodd (15 games, 51 TDs)	N/A	2009
YARDS IN A CAREER			
10,640	Chas Dodd (53 games)	N/A	2006–9
TOUCHDOWNS IN A GAME			
8	Anthony Johnson	T.L. Hanna High School	2001
TOUCHDOWNS IN A SEASON			
39	Willy Korn	N/A	2006
TOUCHDOWNS IN A CAREER			
123	Willy Korn	N/A	2003–6

All-Time Records

RECORD

Amount	Name	Opponent	Year

MOST INTERCEPTIONS THROWN IN A GAME

| 6 | Archie Irby | Northwestern High School | 1987 |

MOST INTERCEPTIONS THROWN IN A SEASON

| 25 | Willy Korn | N/A | 2006 |

MOST INTERCEPTIONS THROWN IN A CAREER

| 40 | Archie Irby | N/A | 1985–7 |

LONGEST PASS COMPLETION

| 97 yards | Archie Irby | J.L. Mann High School | 1987 |

LONGEST TOUCHDOWN PASS

| 97 yards | Archie Irby | J.L. Mann High School | 1987 |

Receiving

RECORD

Amount	Name	Opponent	Year

MOST RECEPTIONS IN A GAME

| 11 | Kelvin Richardson | Gaffney High School | 1984 |

MOST RECEPTIONS IN A SEASON

| 97 | Kelvin Richardson | N/A | 1984 |

MOST RECEPTIONS IN A CAREER

| 147 | Kelvin Richardson | N/A | 1982–4 |

MOST TOUCHDOWN RECEPTIONS IN A GAME

| 4 | Durell Robinson | Eastside High School | 1998 |
| 4 | Jamar Wright | Easley High School | 2003 |

RECORD

Amount	Name	Opponent	Year

MOST TOUCHDOWN RECEPTIONS IN A SEASON

23	Durell Robinson	N/A	1998

MOST TOUCHDOWN RECEPTIONS IN A CAREER

41	Durell Robinson	N/A	1996–8

MOST YARDS RECEIVING IN A GAME

232	Durell Robinson	Eastside High School	1998

MOST YARDS RECEIVING IN A SEASON

1,824	Jamar Wright	N/A	2003

MOST YARDS RECEIVING IN A CAREER

2,626	Jamar Wright	N/A	2001–3

LONGEST PASS RECEPTION

97 yards	Fred Davis	J.L. Mann High School	1987

LONGEST TOUCHDOWN RECEPTION

97 yards	Fred Davis	J.L. Mann High School	1987

Scoring

RECORD

Amount	Name	Opponent	Year

MOST EXTRA POINTS IN A GAME

9	Jonathan Bridwell	Eastside High School	1998

MOST EXTRA POINTS IN A SEASON (STATE RECORD)

93	Kaleb Patterson	N/A	2004

All-Time Records

RECORD

Amount	Name	Opponent	Year

MOST EXTRA POINTS IN A CAREER

| 146 | Brian Sanchez | N/A | 2001–3 |

MOST POINTS IN A GAME

26	Everette Dempsey	Laurens High School	1956
24	Durell Robinson	Eastside High School	1998
24	Willy Korn	Greenwood High School	2005

MOST POINTS IN A SEASON

| 220 | Marcus Lattimore | N/A | 2009 |

MOST POINTS IN A CAREER

| 636 | Marcus Lattimore | N/A | 2006–9 |

MOST FIELD GOALS IN A SEASON

| 13 | Travis Harrison | N/A | 1986 |
| 13 | David Picone | N/A | 2000 |

MOST FIELD GOALS IN A CAREER

| 24 | Travis Harrison | N/A | 1986–8 |

LONGEST FIELD GOAL

| 47 yards | Jordan Miller | Pahokee High School (FL) | 2008 |
| 47 yards | Brian Sanchez | Laurens High School | 2002 |

MOST POINTS (KICK SCORING) IN A SEASON

| 108 | Kaleb Patterson | N/A | 2009 |

MOST POINTS (KICK SCORING) IN A CAREER

| 212 | Brian Sanchez | N/A | 2001–3 |

MOST TOUCHDOWNS IN A GAME

| 4 | Marcus Lattimore | Sumter High School | 2008 |

Special Teams

RECORD

Amount	Name	Opponent	Year

LONGEST PUNT

72	Trey Still	Spartanburg High School	1996

MOST PUNT RETURN YARDS IN A SEASON

343	Nick Jones	N/A	2008

LONGEST KICKOFF RETURN FOR A TOUCHDOWN

93 yards	Scotty Simmons	Woodmont High School	1983

BEST KICKOFF RETURN AVERAGE IN A SEASON

52 yards	Jamey Ballanger	N/A	1995

FEWEST PUNTS IN A SEASON

12 in 15 games		N/A	N/A

Defense

RECORD

Amount	Name	Opponent	Year

MOST INTERCEPTIONS IN A SEASON

13	Scotty Simmons	N/A	1983

MOST INTERCEPTIONS IN A CAREER

20	Fred Foster	N/A	1997

LONGEST INTERCEPTION RETURN FOR A TOUCHDOWN

97 yards	Fred Foster	N/A	1997

MOST FUMBLE RECOVERIES IN A SEASON

5	Everett Dawkins	N/A	2007

RECORD			
Amount	**Name**	**Opponent**	**Year**

LONGEST FUMBLE RETURN FOR A TOUCHDOWN
| 98 yards | Larry Roberson | N/A | 1969 |

MOST SACKS IN A SEASON
| 21 | Dexter Young | N/A | 2004 |

BYRNES TEAM RECORDS

MOST WINS IN A SEASON: 15 in 2003, 2005 and 2007
MOST WINS IN A REGULAR SEASON: 11 in 2003, 2005 and 2007
MOST CONSECUTIVE WINS: 32 in 2004–6
MOST LOSSES IN A SEASON: 11 in 1996
MOST LOSSES IN A ROW: 7 in 1999
WORST OVERALL RECORD: 1–11 in 1996
FEWEST WINS IN A SEASON: 1 in 1996
MOST CONSECUTIVE GAMES WITHOUT BEING SHUT OUT: 147 from 1999–2009
MOST CONSECUTIVE SHUTOUTS, DEFENSIVELY: 5 in 1976

Defensive Records

FEWEST POINTS ALLOWED IN A SEASON: 13 in 1960 (10 games); 49 in 1976 (14 games)
MOST SHUTOUTS IN A SEASON: 9 in 1976 (14 games); 8 in 1960 (10 games)
MOST POINTS ALLOWED IN A GAME: 70 in 1996 versus Northwestern High School
MOST POINTS ALLOWED IN A SEASON: 357 in 1995
MOST PUNTS FORCED IN A SEASON: 75 in 1983
FEWEST YARDS OF TOTAL OFFENSE ALLOWED IN A SEASON: 1,490 in 1983 (12 games)
MOST PASSES INTERCEPTED IN A SEASON: 43 in 1986 (14 games)

FEWEST TOUCHDOWN PASSES ALLOWED IN A SEASON: 0 in 1960
FEWEST PASSING YARDS ALLOWED IN A SEASON: 809 in 1983 (12 games)
FEWEST PASSING YARDS ALLOWED IN A GAME: 0 in 2003 versus Laurens
  High School
FEWEST PASSES COMPLETED IN A SEASON: 62 in 1983 (12 games); 78 in
  1982 (14 games)
FEWEST PASSING COMPLETIONS ALLOWED IN A GAME: 0 in 2002 versus
  Mauldin High School
FEWEST RUSHING TOUCHDOWNS ALLOWED IN A SEASON: 0 in 1960 (10
  games); 1 in 1985 (14 games)
FEWEST RUSHING PLAYS ALLOWED IN A SEASON: 320 in 1983 (12 games)
MOST FUMBLES CAUSED IN A SEASON: 36 in 1982
MOST FUMBLES RECOVERED IN A SEASON: 26 in 1986
FEWEST RUSHING YARDS ALLOWED IN A GAME: 52 in 2008 versus Boiling
  Springs High School
MOST TURNOVERS ALLOWED IN A GAME: 8 versus T.L. Hanna High
  School in 2000
MOST INTERCEPTIONS IN A GAME: 6 versus T.L. Hanna High School
  in 2000

Miscellaneous

MOST PENALTIES IN A SEASON: 105 in 1998
MOST YARDS PENALIZED IN A SEASON: 979 in 1998
MOST PUNTS IN A SEASON: 63 in 1982
BEST PUNT AVERAGE IN A SEASON: 43.8 in 1977 and 38 in 1995

Team Offense Records

TOTAL YARDS IN A SEASON: 8,111 in 2005 (15 games)
TOTAL YARDS IN A GAME: 670 in 1998 versus Eastside High School
MOST PLAYS IN A GAME: 93 in 2005 versus Dorman High School
MOST PLAYS IN A SEASON: 943 in 2005; 910 in 2009
MOST POINTS SCORED IN A GAME: 85 in 2009 versus Woodland High
  School

All-Time Records

MOST POINTS SCORED IN A REGULAR SEASON: 476 in 2006

MOST POINTS SCORED OVERALL: 777 in 2005 (15 games); 767 in 2009 (15 games)

MOST FIRST DOWNS IN A GAME: 31 in 2005 versus Dorman High School

MOST FUMBLES LOST IN A SEASON: 18 in 1999

MOST YARDS RUSHING IN A GAME: 444 in 1997 versus Greer High School

MOST YARDS RUSHING IN A SEASON: 3,611 in 1976

MOST RUSHING ATTEMPTS IN A GAME: 53 in 1982 versus Riverside High School

MOST RUSHING ATTEMPTS IN A SEASON: 569 in 1982

MOST RUSHING TOUCHDOWNS IN A GAME: 7 in 1968 versus Chapman High School

MOST RUSHING TOUCHDOWNS IN A SEASON: 43 in 2003

MOST PASSING YARDS IN A GAME: 600 in 2005 versus Eastside High School

MOST PASSING YARDS IN A SEASON: 3,988 in 2003 (15 games)

MOST PASS COMPLETIONS IN A GAME: 34 in 1992 versus Mauldin High School

MOST PASS COMPLETIONS IN A SEASON: 293 in 2004

MOST PASS ATTEMPTS IN A GAME: 53 in 1986 versus Union High School

MOST PASS ATTEMPTS IN A SEASON: 546 in 2005

MOST INTERCEPTIONS THROWN IN A GAME: 6 in 1986 versus Gaffney High School

MOST INTERCEPTIONS THROWN IN A SEASON: 24 in 1986

MOST TOUCHDOWN PASSES IN A GAME: 6 in 1992 versus Mauldin High School

MOST TOUCHDOWN PASSES IN A SEASON: 73 in 2005

LEAST FUMBLES IN A SEASON: 3 in 2001

CHAPTER 12
BYRNES FOOTBALL
ALL-TIME GREATS

E very year coaches from the Shrine Bowl and North-South All-Star game select the best players from across the state. Below is a list of players that have represented the Rebels during the post season.

SHRINE BOWL SELECTIONS

John Boyette, OT, 1960
Stanley Nelson, OL, 1973
Bill Smith, DE, 1976
Davis Clayton, OL, 1980
Steve Mabry, WR, 1982
Steve Betsill, QB, 1984
James "Bo" Corne, assistant coach, 1984
Kelvin Richardson, WR, 1984
Tony Rogers, RB/LB, 1985
Ray Frost, DT, 1986
Mike Zimmerman, OG, 1989
Courtney Henderson, DB, 1994

John Paul Rogers, OT, 1994
Durell Robinson, WR, 1998
Ben Hall, TE, 2000
Anthony Johnson, QB, 2001
Terrell Allen, WR, 2002
Jake Ravan, C, 2002
Trey Elder, QB, 2003
Jamar Wright, WR, 2003
Reynaldo Hunter, WR, 2004
Trey Bailey, OL, 2004
Prince Miller, DB, 2005
Matt Quinn, WR, 2005
Bobby Bentley, coach, 2005
Stanley Hunter, LB/DE, 2006
Willy Korn, QB, 2006
Everett Dawkins, DL, 2007
Cartier Rice, DB, 2007
Daniel Cleveland, LB, 2008
Justin Bright, DB, 2008

NORTH-SOUTH COACHES' ALL-STAR SELECTIONS

Gene Dillard, OL, 1964
J.T. Williams, DL, 1972 (Defensive MVP)
Steve Durham, DT, 1976
William Meadows, E, 1978
James Glenn, DL, 1979 (Defensive MVP)
Jeff Jones, CB, 1979
Dean Jones, DT, 1981
Scott Revels, C, 1982
Bobby Jackson, FB, 1983
Jay Boland, C, 1984
Scott Simmons, CB, 1984
Bobby Bentley, QB, 1985

Barry Frost, OG, 1985
Kevin Murphy, SS, 1985
Archie Irby, QB, 1987
Tony Pearson, C, 1987
Fred Davis, WR, 1988
Dan Rogers, OG, 1988
Rufus Glenn, DT, 1991 (Defensive MVP)
Abdul Davis, WR, 1993 (Offensive MVP)
Dondre Holcombe, WR, 1997
Tony Lane, QB, 1998
Derrick Smith, RB, 1998
Brandon Peake, C, 2000
Travis Anderson, WR, 2001
Adrian Miller, DB, 2001
Bradley Robinson, WR, 2002
John Talley, DB, 2002
Troy James, OL, 2003
Ben Williams, LB, 2003
Bobby Bentley, coach, 2003
Freddie Brown, WR, 2004
Dexter Young, DE, 2004
Rick Scott, assistant coach, 2004
Steve Kennette, assistant coach, 2004
Jamar Anderson, WR, 2005
Craig Brewton LB, 2005
Chad Deihl, OL/LB, 2006
Curt Thompson, DB, 2007
Randall Hawkins, WR, 2007
Jamie Dunaway, OL, 2008

SOURCES

Hughes, Nell, and Fredrick Tucker. *A Pictoral History of Old Duncan*. Greenville, SC: "A" Press, 1998.

Hughes, Woodrow Wilson. *A History of Duncan, South Carolina*. Greenville, SC: Furman University, 1955.

Spartanburg Herald. "Byrnes Tied," September 10, 1955.

————. "Byrnes vs. Clover," September 9, 1955.

————. "District Five wins by 7–6 Margin over District Two," September 26, 1952.

————. "Duncan Out to Better Record with Big Team," September 17, 1949.

————. "Florence Chapel Opens Season," September 24, 1955.

————. "W-L-T to Field Husky, Veteran Football Squad," September 17, 1949.

ABOUT THE AUTHOR

Zachary David Johnson, Byrnes class of 1999, is a lifelong resident of District 5, which is where his father's family has lived for generations. He is married to his high school sweetheart, Felicia, who was also a member of the Byrnes class of 1999. They have one son, Campbell David Johnson. Zach is an educator and coach.